TWAYNE'S WORLD AUTHORS SERIES
A Survey of the World's Literature

HUNGARY

Enikö Molnár Basa, American University
EDITOR

Kálmán Mikszáth

TWAS 462

Kálmán Mikszáth

KÁLMÁN MIKSZÁTH

By STEVEN C. SCHEER

Saint Meinrad College

TWAYNE PUBLISHERS
A DIVISION OF G. K. HALL & CO., BOSTON

First Printing

Library of Congress Cataloging in Publication Data

Scheer, Steven C 1941–
Kálmán Mikszáth.

(Twayne's world authors series ; TWAS 462 : Hungary)
Bibliography: p. 155–58.
Includes index.
1. Mikszáth, Kálmán, 1847–1910—Criticism and interpretation.
PH3281.M6Z87 894'.511'32 77-7896
ISBN 0-8057-6299-X

MANUFACTURED IN THE UNITED STATES OF AMERICA

For my Mother

Contents

About the Author

Steven C. Scheer was born on January 2, 1941 in Budapest, Hungary. He earned an A.B. and an A.M. from John Carroll University, both in English, and then an M.A. and a Ph.D. in American literature from The Johns Hopkins University. He is presently an Assistant Professor of English at Saint Meinrad College, in St. Meinrad, Indiana, where he teaches courses in British and American fiction and criticism. *Kálmán Mikszáth* is his first book. He is currently at work on a revision of his dissertation which deals with aspects of metafiction in Hawthorne, Melville, and Twain.

Preface

A "metaphor for the act of reading" (Paul de Man), criticism is at best an attempt to render explicit what is implicit in the text. This is never an easy enterprise, but since Hungarian is not one of the frequently studied literatures in the English-speaking world, the task of writing a critical-analytical book on Mikszáth posed some special problems. The most conspicuous of these was that under no circumstances could I permit myself the luxury of assuming familiarity with Mikszáth's works on the part of the readers for whom this study is intended. This meant that I had to try to strike a reasonable balance between necessary plot summaries and the equally necessary critical commentary. While writing this book I did, in fact, make a conscious effort to place myself in the position of a reader who knows no Hungarian but who would nevertheless like to know something about Hungarian literature, particularly about Mikszáth. At the same time, I also tried to keep the level of discussion at a relatively high level of literacy to make the reading of this book worth the while of the advanced Mikszáth scholar as well. In this way I hope I have been able to achieve a compromise between introducing Mikszáth to those of my readers who are seeking introduction and providing some new insights for those readers who are familiar with many or most of the works discussed in the pages which follow.

In an attempt to keep my focus on Mikszáth's works and on the special problems that his works have generated, I kept the historical and biographical background to a minimum. The chapter on his life and times is merely intended to show the world in which Mikszáth lived and worked, and to throw some light on the personality of the author which is indirectly but indubitably present in the narrators who tell the stories of his novels. Otherwise the emphasis in this book is on Mikszáth's novels and on the controversial question of his "Realism." I hope that the unobtrusive application of certain Structuralistic tenets to an interpretation of Mikszáth's stories and novels will prove useful and self-justifying in the long run. Mikszáth's works are particularly inviting to anyone interested in the thematics of fiction and in the always fascinating question of the relationship between the fictive and the real. In giving relatively detailed accounts of what actually happens in representative stories and in nearly all the novels, I hope I have been able to show Mikszáth's considerable contribution to the question of metafiction. Those familiar with his works will find, I believe, that in my interpretation of the novels, as well as in my discussion of Mikszáth's "Realism," I have gone beyond the present state of Mikszáth criticism and that this new look at some old problems is not at all unwarranted. Both the works in question and recent developments in criticism demanded it.

Notwithstanding these virtues of commission (of which the reader will have to be the ultimate judge), those familiar with Mikszáth may well object that many of his excellent shorter works have not even been mentioned. Besides invoking the obligatory excuse of limited space, all I can say in my behalf here is that Mikszáth is primarily a novelist and that his shorter works do not appreciably differ from his longer ones. In the pages which follow, specific stories may go unnoted, but the recurrent themes and evolving narrative techniques that occupy the interior dynamics of these stories do not. In the final analysis, this book attempts to give a total picture of Mikszáth's development as a writer and a complete account of the evolution of his thematic preoccupations. Treating more of his shorter works in detail could have run the risk of redundancy.

STEVEN C. SCHEER

Evansville, Indiana

Acknowledgments

I wish to acknowledge my gratitude to Magyar Helikon, a subsidiary of Európa Könyvkiadó, for the generous permission to quote from the works of Kálmán Mikszáth. I would also like to thank Akadémiai Kiadó for permission to quote from the Mikszáth chapter in *A magyar irodalom története: 1849–1905*, edited by István Sötér. Finally, I wish to acknowledge my indebtedness to Doris Verkamp who has been more than a typist and whose sharp eye for error has been a source of constant enlightenment.

Chronology

1847 Kálmán Mikszáth born in Nográd County, January 16.

1857–1863 Attends *gimnázium* at Rimaszombat.

1863–1866 Continues *gimnázium* at Selmec. Graduates at end of this period.

1866–1870 Studies law in Budapest.

1870–1872 Works as jurist for Mihály Mauks, chief administrator of Nográd County, Mikszáth's future father-in-law.

1872 Asks for Ilona Mauks's hand in marriage and is refused.

1873 Runs for political office in Nográd County and is defeated. Marries Ilona Mauks, without parental permission, in Budapest. Father, János Mikszáth, dies, April 18. Mother, née Mária Veres, dies, July 19. Mikszáth sells family lands and returns to Budapest in November to realize his ambitions as a writer.

1874 Death of infant son. Publication of *Elbeszélések*, 2 vols., at his own expense.

1875 Wife, Ilona, returns to Nográd County because of illness. Mikszáth asks wife for a divorce.

1876–1878 Years of poverty and hardship.

1878–1880 Works for *Szegedi Napló* at Szeged.

1879 Publication of pamphlet about great flood of Szeged; first important social critique.

1880 December, returns to Budapest where he assumes assistant editorship of *Pesti Hirlap*.

1881 Publication of *A tót atyafiak*. Election to Petöfi and Kisfaludy Circles.

1882 Publication of *A jó palócok*. Begins writing parliamentary sketches. December, remarries his former wife.

1882–1883 Serial publication of the novel, *Nemzetes uraimék*.

1885 Publication of *Két koldusdiák*, short historical novel for juvenile audience.

1887 Becomes member of the Liberal Party (also known as the Government Party).

1889 Publication of *A beszélö köntös*, another short historical novel for juvenile audiences, and of *A tekintetes vármegye*, political sketches. Election to Hungarian Academy. Death of János, Mikszáth's three-year-old son.

1892 Becomes Parliamentary Representative of Fogaras in remote Southeastern Transylvania.

1894 Publication of *Beszterce ostroma*.

1895–1898 Publication of important novels: *Szent Péter esernyöje* (1895); *Prakovszky, a siket kovács* (1895–96); *Két választás Magyarországon* (1896–97); *Új Zrinyiász* (1898).

1900 Publication of *Különös házasság*.

1901–1904 Publication of short novels: *A szelistyei asszonyok* (1901); *Akli Miklós* (1903); *A vén gazember* (1904).

1906–1907 Publication of *A Noszty fiú esete Tóth Marival*.

1907 Publication of *Jókai Mór élete és kora*, a biographical novel.

1908–1910 Serial publication of *A fekete város*.

1909 Contracts pneumonia and almost dies.

1910 Grand Celebration in honor of fortieth anniversary of Mikszáth's career as a writer, May 16. Death of Mikszáth, May 28.

CHAPTER 1

Life and Times

I *The Historic Background*

KÁLMÁN Mikszáth's life could easily be taken for the plot of one of his own novels. This is so, in part, because of the historic forces that shaped both the destiny of Hungary and the creative life of one of her most distinguished novelists. Mikszáth was born into the turbulent days of Hungary's War of Independence, grew up in the Era of Absolutism, the so-called Bach Period, and became a writer in Compromise Hungary, the Hungary of the Dual Monarchy. All of his mature works were, in fact, written during the time of the Austro-Hungarian Empire (1867–1918). For this reason it is essential to outline, however briefly, the historic events without which Mikszáth's works may not be properly understood and his particular blend of Romanticism and Realism not adequately appreciated.[1]

The war between Austria and Hungary broke out in 1849 when Mikszáth was hardly out of the cradle. After centuries of stagnation, first under Turkish then under Habsburg domination, Hungary, under the leadership of Lajos Kossuth and the followers of the Revolution of 1848, submitted a declaration of independence to the Austrian emperor. At first the Hungarian army, spurred by the fiery rhetoric of Kossuth and guided by the military genius of Arthur Görgei, was able to outmaneuver the Austrian forces and even to strike some spectacular victories. Shortly after his having been called to power, however, Francis Joseph of Austria called on the Russian tzar, Nicholas I, for help. Since the Tzar was afraid that if Hungary's venture were to succeed the Poles would follow suit, he sent large forces into Hungary. Kossuth fled to Turkey, and Görgei surrendered at Világos on August 13, 1849.

The loss of Hungary's bid for independence led to a reign of terror, alternately referred to as the Era of Absolutism or the Bach Period (named after Alexander Bach, the Austrian Minister of the Interior), which lasted for nearly a decade. During this time attempts were made to strip Hungary of her national identity, and it was during this period that Mikszáth received part of his earliest schooling. Kossuth, who spent the rest of his life in exile, had tried valiantly to summon aid for Hungary's ambitions, first to reinstate the independence declared in 1849, then to form a Danubian Federation which would have guaranteed the total cultural and political equality of the minorities (mostly Croatian, Serbian, Romanian, Slovak, and German) who comprised nearly half the population of historic Hungary (including Transylvania). Kossuth was enthusiastically welcomed in England and in the United States, but his dreams of an independent Hungary met with no concrete success. It was, however, Kossuth's rhetoric combined with his highly democratic and radical ideology—in short, the "Spirit of 48"—that played a significant role in Mikszáth's Romanticism. The memory of the glorious past which the subsequent Era of Absolutism was never able to suppress appreciably, or the suppression of which made it all the more appealing, shaped Mikszáth's initial world-view. The "Spirit of 48" was, in fact, the mainstay of the future author's hope for a new Hungary, and it was not until the disillusioning political and moral corruption of the minor nobility, which had once played such a revolutionary role in the nation, that Mikszáth's characteristically urbane satire was to turn bitter and vindictive.

Since the reign of absolutism was unpopular outside as well as inside Hungary, and since the Habsburgs were beset by a host of pressing international threats, a reconciliation between Austria and Hungary seemed more and more promising. Ferenc Deák, the political and legal mastermind of the Compromise *(Ausgleich)* of 1867, insisted on the legality and constitutionality of the so-called April Laws of 1848, which meant that Hungary would once again accept the emperor of Austria as her king. After the Compromise, Hungary regained complete control of her internal affairs. Foreign affairs, defense, as well as international trade were to be jointly administered by the two equal partners. In Hungary itself parliamentary democracy was in the hands of two parties, the Government Party (later called the Liberal Party), which supported the Compromise, and the Party of Independence (later called the Party of Opposition), which remained loyal, at least nominally, to the still self-exiled Kossuth.

The political as well as social and economic life of the country, however, was still beset by contradictions and ambivalences. The role of the middle class was assumed by the minor nobility or gentry, but unfortunately this class was frequently more interested in its own privileges than in the welfare of the nation. The problems posed by the various ethnic groups within the boundaries of historic Hungary were also alarming, but the ruling factions gave little or no thought to these potentially disruptive forces that were already at work so that the frequently maligned and at times unjustly evaluated Magyarization failed. As good as in some ways it was, the problems inherent in the system were later to assert themselves with devastating results, not the least of which was the dismemberment of historic Hungary at the Treaty of Trianon in 1920, ten years after Mikszáth's death. Mikszáth saw much of what was lacking in Compromise Hungary, and toward the end of his life he became increasingly gloomy and pessimistic about the future of his native land, but he saw no way out of the ever rising negative forces, both internal and external, that were to plunge the reluctant and uneasy partner of Austria into World War I.

II *The Making of a Writer*

Mikszáth was born on January 16, 1847, at Szklabonya in Nográd County.[2] The village of his birth was subsequently renamed Mikszáthfalva in honor of its most distinguished native son. His father, János Mikszáth, was a farmer and at times an innkeeper, even a butcher. The family was on the borderline between minor nobility and peasantry and looked back to days when its forebears were Protestant ministers. Mikszáth was a weak child, frequently bedridden. His first introduction to literature came via folktales as narrated by the well-known storytellers of the region whom his father was wont to hire whenever young Kálmán was ailing. It is, perhaps, thanks to his mother, née Mária Veres, that Mikszáth did not take over the family farm upon graduation from the *gimnázium*. As tradition has it, one of his mother's acquaintances had once prophesied that the boy would grow up to be a great man. In this case the prophecy was fulfilled despite the fact that as a student

Mikszáth showed little or no promise. At the age of ten he was enrolled in the old Protestant *gimnázium* of Rimaszombat where he completed the first six years of his studies. In 1863 he continued his schooling at Selmec where Sándor Petöfi (1823–49), the great Hungarian poet, had also been a student not long before. Mikszáth's teachers at both schools included men who had fought under Kossuth's banner so that the "Spirit of 48" was certainly pervasive in the life of the future writer at this time. Petöfi himself, certainly the most eminent alumnus of the *gimnázium* at Selmec, died (or at least disappeared) on a battlefield in Transylvania in the fall of 1849.

Although not an exceptional student, Mikszáth was certainly a mischievous one. A characteristic episode dating from his schooldays is prefigurative of his subsequent humor. At one point the young Kálmán had formed a mushroom out of the soft inside of a loaf of bread, dried it, and presented it to his biology teacher as some sort of rare and petrified relic from a prehistoric age. The deception was a success, at least temporarily. Another such episode, which may throw some light on Mikszáth's lifelong fondness for eccentrics, is recorded in a brief autobiographical sketch, "Hogy lettem iróvá" ("How I Became a Writer"). Having always had trouble with his writing, young Mikszáth once plagiarized a story about King Mátyás. The teacher noticed it, but instead of reprimanding him, he told the young plagiarist to be sure to write like that from then on. By the time he was working as a young jurist for his future father-in-law, Mikszáth's style had certainly improved. Ironically, however (and this irony is also characteristic of typical Mikszáth plots to come), this instance was a failure of sorts, for his colleagues severely criticized his first brief, because it was written in a simple and readily comprehensible language instead of the customarily convoluted legalese.

After graduating from the *gimnázium*, Mikszáth moved to Budapest where he studied law for a period of four years. Little is known of these years of his life except that it was about this time, that Mikszáth began to write in earnest. The writings from this period tend to be philosophical and learned, full of quotations from foreign languages and erudite dissertations. His first published work is a little essay on the nature of witticisms and compliments (1869) in which the young Mikszáth gives the kind of recommendation he himself was to follow, for the most part, in his humorous and satiric works: namely, never to allow a witticism to wound. By the time of his return to his native region, where for the next two years he was to work as a jurist for Mihály Mauks, the chief administrative officer of Nográd County, Mikszáth was himself a very witty, albeit still awkward, youth. It was, in fact, thanks to his wit that Ilona, his employer's daughter and his own future wife, noticed him at all. The love that was soon to grow between them was founded on their shared love for literature, more specifically on their common response to the works of Victor Hugo and Charles Dickens and to Mór Jókai, the Hungarian author. Not that Mikszáth's penchant for practical jokes had disappeared completely. At one point, for example, the young jurist had slipped among a pile of documents a sheet on which the undersigned promises to give his daughter, Ilona Mauks, to Kálmán Mikszáth within a year. Mihály Mauks, of course, unwittingly signed this "legally binding" document.

Although Ilona's father did not want to give his daughter to a would-be writer, for he felt that this calling would probably never provide a married couple with an adequate living, he did offer Mikszáth a chance to run for political office. But by this time Mikszáth's dream of becoming a writer was too strong. He moved to Budapest for the second time, this time with the intention of fulfilling that dream. Here he met Ilona again and in the spring of 1873 married her without parental consent. When his mother died on July 19 of the same year, a victim of a cholera epidemic, Mikszáth was once more compelled to return to his native region (his father having died earlier that same year of a respiratory ailment), and take over the family farm. But farming suited him no better than the profession of law, and by the end of the same year he had sold his family property and, once again, returned to Budapest. In 1874, in accordance with his ambitions as a writer, he published his first book at his own expense, a collection of tales in two volumes. *Elbeszélések (Short Narratives)*, however, did not bring the desired success; it merely depleted his savings. It was in this same year that Mikszáth's first child was born, but almost as if to repeat the fate of the child of its father's imagination, it died shortly thereafter. Then Ilona herself became ill and was forced to return to her ancestral home where she intended to recuperate for an indefinite period of time.

These were bleak times for Mikszáth. His income from the various and sundry papers he was working for was not even enough to keep him above what we would today call the poverty line. His wife was used to better days, and his inability to earn more money had pushed Mikszáth to the brink of despair. It seemed that his father-in-law's reservations were well taken. By the end of 1875 Mikszáth had made a risky but firm decision in which he was going to gamble both with his and his wife's future happiness. In December of that year he wrote his wife and asked her for a divorce. He told her how desperately he had tried to turn the tide of their ill fortune, but to no avail. "Perhaps I could have become an official," he went on, "and thus slowly destroy you as well as myself in a life not suited for me . . . but I know you well enough to know that you would not want this. I must continue on the course I have begun, which could either raise me high or lower me completely. And I have not the heart to drag you with me, should my course continue downward."[3] His wife's response to this letter was noble and self-abnegating. She stated that she could not imagine that their present poverty should be allowed to separate them. That is not what she had promised at the altar. She went on to promise to go on a tighter budget, to sell her jewelry, and to work. However his wife's response may have affected Mikszáth, it is clear that he could not endure to see his wife go on suffering privations for his sake, even if she were willing to do so. In his next letter, therefore, Mikszáth resorted to a lie. "You have forced me to tell you the truth," he wrote, "I love another. I know this is terrible, but I cannot help it. It is a matter of fate."[4] To this his wife's simple response was to agree to a divorce and to promise never to bother him again.

In 1878 Mikszáth received an invitation from Szeged, the largest city in Southeastern Hungary, on the banks of the Tisza. Here he worked for the *Szegedi Napló (Szeged Daily)* for a period of two years. This second apprenticeship seems to have done him a world of good. His articles and editorials, written in sympathy with the Party of Independence, earned him popularity, at least on the local level. His attacks on the ineffective bureaucracy had increased his fame, and by the time he published the pamphlet, *Szeged pusztulása (The Destruction of Szeged;* 1879), his antiestablishment stance had also taken on the kind of gently satiric yet biting social critique his fiction was soon to exploit so successfully. He had also published more stories during this time.

In 1880, he returned to Budapest to become assistant editor of *Ország-Világ (Nation-World)* and later of *Pesti Hirlap (Budapest Gazette)* with which he was to remain associated for nearly twenty years. The next two years saw his rise to long-awaited national acclaim, for with the publication of *A tót atyafiak (Our Slovak Kinfolk)* and of *A jó palócok (The Good Palóc People)*, two collections of stories based on his recollections of his native region, the tide had finally, and apparently irrevocably, turned. Mikszáth was once again in a position to address his wife: "if you have not yet married, *I would now like to marry you for the second time.*"[5] His wife's response was happy but cautious. She was happy to learn at long last that her ex-husband's final letter to her many years before was not true, but she could not imagine that their future at this time had anything more in it than a willingness to remember their past as "that beautiful dream of spring which had passed away forever."[6] This tenderly distant response notwithstanding, the year which saw the reopening of their correspondence was also to witness their remarriage.

III *The Years of Fame and Success*

By now it should be clear why I began this chapter with the statement that Mikszáth's life is certainly worthy of the plot of one of his own novels. But the story is not yet over. Even though the remainder of his life was to be devoid of the kind of romanticism that had characterized the story of his marriage, it was not going to be devoid of the stuff of which his novels were to be made. Paradoxically, his next popular success was not to come from his fiction but from his political sketches. The *Pesti Hirlap* had been running a column of parliamentary reports. When the man in charge of this column became ill, the editor urged Mikszáth to take it over temporarily. He did this so reluctantly that he wrote the first column without even attending the parliamentary session of which it was supposedly an eyewitness report. Because he had written the report in a lively, satiric tone, however, the column had suddenly become an instant success.

Thereafter Mikszáth was to write parliamentary sketches for nearly ten years, during which time his political affiliation underwent substantial changes. His first sketches were against the Liberal Party, since at this time his sympathies were still with the Party of the Opposition. Slowly, however, he was to vest more and more hope in Kálmán Tisza, the leader of the liberals. But it should be noted that the popularity of his parliamentary sketches transcended their author's political leanings. This was so because Mikszáth himself was more apartisan than not when it came to a consideration of "truth" or "right." Furthermore, he was more interested in personalities than in issues, and wherever he saw abuses, instances of bureaucratic stalemate, or worse, manifestations of corruption or moral turpitude, his pen went to work and it worked with merciless wit yet with compassion and a willingness to forgive. In this way Mikszáth's parliamentary sketches accomplished two things: they made his name synonymous with considerable political power, while they also made it possible for their author to demystify politics even as he was later to deintoxicate Romanticism.

The honors that came his way were never able to corrupt him. This will be borne out again and again by the works I will be examining in the chapters which follow this one. In fact, what Coleridge had once stated of Shakespeare, "such as the life is, such is the form," can equally well be said of Mikszáth, but with a slight modification: such as the man is, such is the work. In 1881 Mikszáth was elected both to the Petöfi and to the Kisfaludy Circles (important literary societies). A few years later he was also invited to join the distinguished ranks of the Hungarian Academy. Meanwhile, he was to receive political office as well. Having become a member of the Liberal Party in 1887, in 1892 Mikszáth also became the parliamentary representative of Fogaras, a remote district in Southeastern Transylvania, which position (his sole political office) he was to hold for the rest of his life. But social and political honors notwithstanding, Mikszáth had remained a simple family man. Although he was enamored of cards and of fine foods, he disliked high society and its excessively formalized rituals. His family life had also remained exemplary, which, as one of his biographers has pointed out, is a rarity, especially among artists and writers. The one domestic tragedy that was to leave a profound mark on his mental make-up was the death of his three-year-old son in 1889. His two other sons, Kálmán, Jr. and Albert, became men of letters; the first an eminent lawyer and political essayist, the second a journalist.

Having risen to fame for a second time with his political sketches, in 1882–83 Mikszáth finally turned to the novel with the serial publication of *Mácsik, a nagyerejü (Mácsik, the Mighty)* which was to appear in book form in 1884 under the title of *Nemzetes uraimék (Our Honorable Gentlefolk).* This first novel bears witness to Mikszáth's long apprenticeship as a short-story writer and journalist.

It is so loosely constructed that the series of episodes which constitute it give it the impression of forced unity. Its thematic preoccupation, however, had already begun the deintoxication of Romanticism Mikszáth inherited from Jókai, the most eminent Hungarian novelist of the day. Jókai's tradition is the tradition of the Romantic fabulator. Brought up in the "Spirit of 48," Jókai was never able to transcend the magic of his own immediate past. His numerous novels constantly recreate the idealistic and idealized struggles of the generation of the War of Independence in such a way that the reader almost gets the impression that this war was never really lost, that the spirit that made it possible is still alive, and that it is merely waiting for an opportunity to reassert itself. Mikszáth's Romanticism was almost from the beginning a Romanticism of disillusionment. In his works the ideal, the romantic, the way things should be, in short, are constantly being contrasted with the real, with the way things really are. This discrepancy is already present in *Nemzetes uraimék*. Mácsik gets involved in a hopeless legal suit to regain an entire county for the family that had once owned it. In the end, when the War of Independence comes, the broken Mácsik revives himself to die for the glorious cause. This indicates that Mikszáth was profoundly influenced both by Jókai and the "Spirit of 48," that he did look back with nostalgia to the days when the nobility, moved by a spirit of genuinely self-abnegating patriotism, attempted heroic things. What distinguishes Mikszáth is that he saw the irreconcilable gap between the "romantic" and the "real," between, in short, the poetic and the prosaic.

The world of Mikszáth's novels is thus created by the ever renewed tension that exists between the ideal and the real. Although his narrators are capable of entertaining the ideal as though it were the real, and the real as though it could become the ideal at any moment, they never share the illusions of the characters, who frequently do not or cannot differentiate between these two opposing forces. Much depends on the ultimate model. Those Mikszáth characters who insist on using the ideal as their model are either heroic or pathetic, perhaps even foolish, but always in an endearing way, whereas those characters who use the real as their ideal (relatively few in number) are usually selfish or materialistic.

Attempts by Mikszáth's critics to differentiate sharply between the various stages of Mikszáth's development are almost always disappointing. They seem to create the Mikszáth whose stages they thus categorize. One recent attempt, for example, insists that the early Mikszáth, as exemplified by the stories of *A tót atyafiak (Our Slovak Kinfolk)* and *A jó palócok, (The Good Palóc People)* is idyllic. In these stories Mikszáth idealizes the folk. In this early period, as many of his critics have noted, the adult Mikszáth recreates his own childhood impressions of the peasantry, impressions at once idealized and authentic. Mikszáth's second stage is said to be permeated by an overriding sense of irony. The best work of his ironic period includes such novels as *Beszterce ostroma (The Siege of Beszterce)* or *Új Zrinyiász (New Zrinyiad)*. These works are heavy with dramatic irony, with the difference between what the characters think and experience and what the narrator (and along with the narrator, the reader) sees and knows. In these novels romantic characters are pitted against a real world, but not necessarily with negative results as far as the attitude of the reader is concerned. More often than not, from the reader's point of view, the loser is not the romantic but the real, and therein, I think, lies the real irony of these works. The third stage is said to be Mikszáth's Realistic stage. The great novels of Mikszáth's final period, *Különös házasság (Strange Marriage), A Noszty fiú esete Tóth Marival (The Noszty Boy's Affair with Mari Tóth)*, and *A fekete város (The Black City)*, are said to be Realistic because they are more critical of the society of the present as well as of the past than any of his previous novels. But, as my detailed analyses of the novels in question will show, these distinct stages are not as sharply differentiated as the particular Mikszáth critic in question seems to imply.[7] Rather than distinct stages, they represent different degrees or emphases of the same basic mode of perception. The idyllic is predominant in the early Mikszáth, while the ironic dominates the middle and the Realistic the late. But all of these different degrees or emphases are present throughout, from beginning to end.

The preceding reflections on Mikszáth's work give, in the final analysis, the best picture of the inner life of the man. After marrying his wife for the second time in 1882, Mikszáth led a life devoid of external excitement, and his activities were confined to the routine of his journalistic and semipolitical work, uninterruptedly punctuated by the steady writing of his stories and novels. But this routine was certainly not dull. The kind of humor that pervades his works apparently also pervaded his everyday existence. The amusing anecdotes about Mikszáth the man are almost as numerous as the amusing anecdotes that keep cropping up in his fiction. I have already mentioned some examples of his youthful mischievousness. The adult Mikszáth was apparently no less mischievous than his adolescent and youthful counterpart. One such characteristic episode was actually responsible for his writing of *Szent Péter esernyöje (St. Peter's Umbrella)*, one of his best early novels which also has the distinction of having captured for its author the feminine portion of the reading public, and which appeared in serial form in the newly established *Új Idők (New Times)* in 1895. József Wolfner, the publisher of the new weekly, had hoped that Mikszáth would contribute a new novel for the paper to assure its success. Since one of Mikszáth's steady cardplaying partners had recently gone on an extended journey, it was agreed that a new novel would be written for the weekly provided that its publisher would agree to fill in for the absent cardplayer. So the publisher played cards, and Mikszáth wrote a new novel.[8]

Another characteristic anecdote is recorded by Mikszáth himself in a typical letter to the editor. *Az Újság (The Newspaper)* had apparently given a distorted version of an episode from his own life in 1905. Mikszáth then contributed a correction subsequently entitled "Az én kritikusom" ("My Own Critic"). In this vignette he tells us that the cook, an old woman at a well-known resort, had hurt her leg and was consequently confined to her bed where she intended to while away her time by reading. As Mikszáth had just arrived with a suitcase full of books, this worthy woman asked him to lend her one. Mikszáth, of course, could not resist the temptation of giving the cook one of his own recently published novels. The old woman immediately put on her spectacles and proceeded to read. After a sentence or two she cast a bewildered look at Mikszáth, then attempted to continue her reading. After another sentence or two, however, she closed the book in desperation and handed it back to its owner, stating that the " 'gentleman' " must have been trying to " 'ridicule' " her. When Mikszáth inquired what she meant by that, her response was simply: " 'Oh, go on. I can write like that myself.' " This, according to Mikszáth, was the greatest compliment he had ever received as a writer. "She had found my style so natural," he states, "that she did not even consider it to be a [real] book" (XV, 379).

Notwithstanding his "natural" style, the public at large did consider his books to be real. Nothing is more indicative of this than the grand celebration given in honor of the fortieth anniversary of Mikszáth's career as a writer, on May 16, 1910. Although at this point Mikszáth was an invalid, having just recuperated from pneumonia the year before, that day must certainly have been one of the happiest in his life. Mikszáth's response to the fanfare and to the numerous speeches in his honor was characteristic of his own endearing humanity and of his perception of and insight into human nature in general. Just as Faulkner had accepted the Nobel Prize not in his own name but in the names of the still struggling young writers, Mikszáth accepted the grand celebration on the basis that it was only partly for him and partly for all the writers who had not yet succeeded but who would undoubtedly succeed in the not too distant future. The most endearing quality of his humanity embodied in his acceptance speech is perhaps best expressed by the following: "I cannot pretend to believe all the praises that were said of me here today, for if they were all true, I would be a veritable miracle. Yet I hope you will not expect me to try to convince you that these praises are not true, for if I were to try and do that, I would be an even greater miracle." Then, authentically moved by the tremendous demonstration of affection his reading public had provided for him, Mikszáth concluded his speech by stating "yet the moment is nevertheless a miraculous one; it is as though I had been fabulating all these years till I myself have become a part of the fable."[9] Mikszáth died twelve days after this celebration, on May 28, 1910. At the time of his death he was working on a new novel that would have clarified Hungary's legal ties to Austria, ties that were soon to be severed by years of bloodshed and unspeakable waste of lives.

CHAPTER 2

The Shorter Works

I *General Characteristics*

FOR a critic interested in statistical evidence, Mikszáth's shorter works would have to take precedence over his novels in that the total number of pages occupied by the former exceed the total number of pages occupied by the latter. Since Mikszáth is nevertheless best known as a novelist, this chapter will merely concentrate on a representative sampling of his short fiction. Although, for the most part, the production of the short stories or novellas runs concurrent with the writing of the novels, Mikszáth's career as a novelist is preceded by a relatively long period of apprenticeship as a short-story writer. An examination of a representative selection of his shorter works, therefore, will not only give the reader some idea of Mikszáth's contribution to this genre but will also serve as an adequate introduction to his novels. Furthermore, since, as a number of his critics have noted, Mikszáth's shorter works do not appreciably differ from his novels in quality,[1] this chapter will also serve as an introduction to Mikszáth's characteristic themes and narrative techniques.

Mikszáth's imagination seems to have been inseparably wedded to the childhood and adolescent impressions of his native region. His early acquaintance with folk and fairy tales seems also to have left a permanent mark on his subsequent creative endeavors. As one of his critics has suggested, in Mikszáth's works fable takes precedence over psychology. For the psychological author character is more important than fable, and the latter exists for the sake of the former. In Mikszáth this is usually the other way around.[2] Yet saying that fable takes precedence over psychology should not be taken to mean that for Mikszáth character is not important. As another of his critics has shown, it is also true to say that for Mikszáth plot is subservient to character. His imagination works with characters, and only when the characters take on a definite shape do the stories which will animate them come to be associated with them.[3] This is borne out by one of Mikszáth's contemporaries who recalls how Mikszáth was in the habit of constantly discussing his works in progress. According to the testimony of this particular critic, each time Mikszáth recounted a story or novel he was thinking about, it became a bit more subtle and sophisticated, and he never started writing until the progress of the whole was relatively clear in his mind.[4] As I shall frequently show in analyses in this as well as in subsequent chapters, for Mikszáth the relationship between fable and character is a crucial one. It is, after all, what a man is that makes him do what he does. But by the same token, what a man does is always a reflection of what he is. This observation applies not only to the characters in Mikszáth's fables, but also to the relationship that exists between the typical Mikszáthian narrator and what this narrator narrates.

In Mikszáth's case the key to this relationship, both between the fable and the character and the fabulator and the fable, is to be found in the writer's special sense of humor. For Mikszáth, humor is a mood that pervades all his works, and what characterizes this mood is a mixture between sadness and gaiety reminiscent of the archetypal tearful clown. His works embody a humorous world-view according to which life is weird and its weirdness is our own creation; at the same time, it is a comedy whose Great Director constantly pokes loving fun at us.[5] As another of his critics has characterized it, for Mikszáth humor is not a means to an end, it is an end in itself. He sees the bitter reality of life and "tries to escape it by dissolving it in humor." He is a skeptic whose humor is itself his world-view. He views man as a victim of his own material interests, his own lusts, and (above all) his own vanity. This view can be seen as at once cynical and wise in that Mikszáth seems to "laugh at the world and at life in order to keep from crying."[6]

This sense of humor coupled with Mikszáth's lifelong indebtedness to the folk and fairy tale leads to an important distinction between Mikszáthian characters in Mikszáthian fables on the one hand, and the typically Mikszáthian narrator and what this narrator narrates on the other. The Mikszáthian narrator never identifies with his characters. And the reader never experiences any difficulty as to which of the characters he is to love or hate, or approve or disapprove of, precisely because of this lack of narratorial identification, or, to put it in positive terms, because of the presence of this narratorial detachment. What the Mikszáthian narrator does is to have the reader identify with him. As a number of his critics have noted, the Mikszáthian narrator is characterized by an easygoing tone, as though he were talking to his readers, "as though there were a living voice . . . [speaking through] the written sentence."[7]

By virtue of the fact that this live narration is strategically combined with what may be termed indirect narration, Mikszáth almost always succeeds in creating a special effect in his readers. This happens not only because the reader is subtly invited to think of himself as an extension of the narrator's knowledge and (above all) observation, but because frequently he is not shown directly what a specific action in a given story is; rather, he is allowed to guess what it must be.[8] This creates a sense of harmony between the telling and that which is told as well as between the teller and his audience, precisely because the audience can see the aforementioned harmony between the telling and that which is told. And this double relationship between the teller and his audience on the one hand, and the telling and the told on the other, stems from the fact that, as one critic has characterized it, Mikszáth's style is at once "radically folkish and nobly literate."[9] Or, to put the matter in a slightly different perspective, it is not really the style per se that is folkish, but the content. That is to say, in Mikszáth there is a perfect harmony between literate language and folkish mentality.[10]

One of the most conspicuous characteristics of Mikszáth's writings (whether his stories or novels are lifted from the world of his contemporaries or from that of the historic past makes little difference here) is the mixture of Romanticism and Realism they tolerate. As I shall frequently have occasion to show hereinafter, this mixture is at times a deliberate confrontation between the Romantic and the Realistic. This is a highly problematic issue in Mikszáth criticism, and at this point I should merely like to bring it to the reader's attention. In the analyses that follow in this as well as in subsequent chapters I shall have more to say about it, and in Chapter 5 I shall deal with this issue specifically and at some length. Let it suffice to say here, therefore, that the conflict between the Romantic and the Realistic in Mikszáth is not a simple matter. At times the Romantic is clearly allowed to triumph over the Realistic, whereas at other times the latter is clearly victorious. Each case has a meaning of its own. This question, then, is at once technical and thematic. On the technical side it is not at all clear whether Mikszáth is primarily a Romanticist or a Realist, whereas on the thematic side it is usually clear as to when the Romantic or when the Realistic view of life is preferred or preferable. Since Mikszáth conceived of literature as a realm where justice and goodness triumph—that is, as a kind of antidote to life[11]—, it would seem safe to say that he was essentially a Romanticist. Since, however, he also saw that Romantic illusions or delusions are detrimental to happiness (as witness his many eccentrics who are defined by such illusions, delusions, or obsessions), it would also seem safe to say that he was essentially a Realist. It is hoped that as this book progresses, this problematic issue will become clearer and clearer.

II *The First Stories*

"Ami a lelket megmérgezi" ("That Which Poisons the Soul"; 1871) is Mikszáth's first published story; it was written in response to a contest for a story about the folk and for the folk. It is essentially a didactic, anti-*betyár* tale. The Hungarian word *betyár* has no exact equivalent in English; it refers to an outlaw who is a combination Robin Hood and political fugitive of sorts who, rather than serve the foreign interests represented by the Habsburgs, hides out in the mountains or in the marshlands of the plains to lead an independent, albeit hardship-ridden, existence. This particular story is a kind of miniature *Don Quixote*. János Kerekes loves to read *betyár* stories, which paint a highly romanticized and idealized picture of the life of the outlaw. János, the son of a peasant, is a talented youth who, notwithstanding his lowly position in life, could easily become a priest or a judge. His "soul," however, is poisoned by the Romantic stories he reads. Even when he grows into a handsome young man and falls in love with a girl of his own station in life, he continues to devour these adventure stories until one day, tempted by the vision generated by the many books he has read, he decides to join a band of outlaws said to be operating in a nearby forest. No sooner does János join up with the outlaws than he regrets his decision. The discrepancy between the Romantic tales he has read and the reality of the life he has chosen for himself makes itself painfully apparent. He abandons the life of the outlaw, spends eight years in the army for penance (the *betyár* usually became an outlaw precisely because he did not want to serve in the army that represented foreign interests), and finally marries the girl he should have married in the first place. Mikszáth projects János as lucky since he has been "able to raise himself after he has fallen." At the end of the story the narrator admonishes his readers to "reflect a little upon this history," for "books are like mushrooms; as good and nourishing as some may be, others may be just as poisonous" (VII, 36).

"Ami a lelket megmérgezi" is permeated by a strong sense of anti-Romanticism. The whole story is one adamant warning against foolish books that glamorize what is in reality unglamorous. The didacticism of "A Lutri" ("The Lottery"; 1872) runs along similar lines. This time the target is the kind of vain dreaming about riches the institution of the lottery encourages. Although full of sentimentality and moralizing, the construction of this story is already typical of the "later" Mikszáth. The ground situation is provided by the dream of an old lady in which the numbers 17, 33, and 74 play a prominent role. Marci Fodros is convinced that the numbers should be played on the lottery. At this point the narrator goes back in time to recount Fodros's own story. For years now Fodros has been slowly gambling his livelihood away. Once he won a small sum, but winning that prize was merely the beginning of his undoing. The get-rich-quick dream inherent in the institution of the lottery became his sole obsession. He kept selling his lands and chattels in order to gamble, while all along he kept hoping for the grand prize that would permanently establish his fortune. At the time the old lady relates her dream, Fodros is on the verge of utter poverty, yet his hopes for riches via the lottery are as high as ever. To play the numbers in question he would have to get an extension from one of his creditors, but this he is not able to accomplish. When the numbers in question do win, Marci Fodros loses his mind.

Fodros then journeys to Budapest with a collection of old lottery slips. He hopes to persuade the king to exchange the old slips for money; in other words, he wants his money back. A fellow townsman, who is a politician and a member of the upper class, takes old Marci Fodros under his protection. The old man undergoes treatment in a mental institution where he completely recovers his senses. Fodros's protector returns the old man to his family and buys the lands old Fodros had previously gambled away, saying that if God was kind enough to give back the old man's sanity, he, Miklós

Szent-Tamássy, can do no more than give back the old man's worldly possessions that he may be a "whole" man again (VII, 121).

This is the core of the plot. Its heavily moralistic tone, which could easily have engulfed the tale in sheer didacticism, is counterbalanced by its narrative technique. Although himself a moralizer, the narrator maintains a satiric detachment. He is not above arguing with his readers or admonishing them for their willingness to delude themselves. At one point, for example, he tells his readers that they are wont to label as "nonsense" those "printed letters" which do not unabashedly praise them "for virtues they do not possess." The issue the narrator raises here is handled ingeniously. He presupposes that his readers would blame "fate" or "misfortune" for all things that happen contrary to their wishes. If a drunk, for instance, "stumbles and breaks his arm," this is to be attributed to his "fate." Here the narrator claims that he cannot permit himself the luxury of "plagiarizing" this notion from his public. He states that he "must tell the truth," and the truth is that "each man is the maker of his own fortune" (VII, 89). The story of Marci Fodros is an illustration of this principle. And the moral of the story is stated explicitly not by the narrator but by Fodros's protector, Miklós Szent-Tamássy (the "saint" [szent] in his name is a clue to his personality). When Szent-Tamássy ceremoniously returns the old man's property, he makes a speech for the benefit of those present. He tells them that " 'this is a sad story . . . but it has a nice moral.' " And the moral is that one should not " 'seek fortune in vain dreams, in empty tales, in the air,' " because fortune can only be found in " 'work' " (VII, 121).

The moral of the Fodros story as formulated by Szent-Tamássy is then placed into a larger context, a context which provides the didactic tone of the whole tale with an additional saving grace. The political followers of Szent-Tamássy publicize the entire affair as an example of their candidate's nobility. His opponents, however, regard it as "unprecedented bribery" in which Szent-Tamássy goes to ridiculous lengths to purchase a favorable vote (VII, 123). It is through the eyes of Szent-Tamássy's political opponent that we see the final part of the story. Filtered through the consciousness of this new character, its didacticism is rendered even more acceptable. When, after some investigation, Szent-Tamássy's political opponent is convinced that the whole affair is an example of authentic humanitarianism, he is forced to exclaim that he is " 'in the land of fairy tales' " (VII, 124), thus implying that the story is too good to be true. In the final analysis, the story becomes an allegory of national restoration. Szent-Tamássy's political opponent makes an explicit connection between the restoration of a man and that of an entire nation (VII, 127). The accomplishment of the one seems to be a guarantee of the potential success of the other. It is on this note that the story ends.

Notwithstanding their technical excellence and the ironic or satiric mode of their narration, these early stories remain highly moralistic and, at times, sentimental to a fault. The humanistic vision which everywhere informs them is too much in the foreground so that their moralistic truth transcends and thus undermines their artistic validity. Their ultimate value lies in their function as markers of the beginning of Mikszáth's development, which will quickly rise to the occasion. Rather than abandoning his humanitarian vision, the "later" Mikszáth will soon find it possible to make his moral vision coincide with his artistic truth. In the world created by his fiction the two remain inseparable, for when there is a change in Mikszáth's outlook it is not a shift away from his basically moral vision but an enlargement of its expanse.

III A tót atyafiak *(1881)*

The publication of *A tót atyafiak (Our Slovak Kinfolk)* was not only Mikszáth's first commercial success, it was also the first authentic literary achievement of his career. The stories contained in the volume are imbued with the magic of folktales. Humor, gentle satire, and ironic detachment are mixed with lyricism and compassion. The heroes of the various stories are usually the sons and daughters of the peasantry, of the people. Although according to one of his critics, Mikszáth's view of the "folk" is highly Romantic and therefore, to a certain extent, distorted,[12] the idyllic quality of the tales, as I shall shortly show, contains anti-Romantic elements, elements that tend to show the detrimental effects of a too Romantic vision of life, of a vision of life especially as it is influenced by the popular fiction of the day. The first story of the volume, "Az aranykisasszony" ("The Golden Maid"), is a veritable fairy tale told as though it were a completely Realistic story. The "live" narration so characteristic of Mikszáth throughout his career is fully realized here. By "live" narration, as indicated earlier in this chapter, I mean the Mikszáthian technique of narrating his stories as though he were telling them to a live audience rather than committing them to paper. This lends to his stories a charm and a unique atmosphere which remains with Mikszáth's narrators, in one form or another, throughout all of his writings.[13]

"Az aranykisasszony" is built around a quadrangular love conflict. Two middle-aged men fall in love with the daughter of a mutual friend. The girl, in order to escape both her suitors, gives her affections to a third man, a youth who, fired by a Romanticism akin to that of heroes in popular fiction, attempts the impossible in order to be honorably deserving of his future happiness. The story ends in limbo. It is clear that the youth has been able to achieve the impossible, but it is also clear that his desires have probably been sidetracked in the attempt.

The story begins with the characterization of the two middle-aged men. The first, Csutkás by name, is a teacher of literature whose single claim to fame lies in the fact that he was once the professor of Sándor Petőfi, the great Hungarian poet. Csutkás believes that his students worship him. It is in fact this by and large self-generated fiction of his students' affection and esteem for him that sustains his self-respect; otherwise Csutkás is a taciturn man. If and when, fired by wine, he does talk, his professorial digressions soon make him so forgetful of his original topic that his talk never gets anywhere. Luppán, the other middle-aged man, is talkative to the point of loquaciousness. He particularly loves to dwell on the tragic death of his wife followed by the untimely death of his children. The narrator hastens to inform his readers that Luppán has never been married and that he has never had children. It appears that Luppán's self-generated fiction still has a foundation in reality in that a girl he had once wanted to marry committed suicide because her parents had objected to the alliance. In the aftermath of this tragedy Luppán himself fell ill, and it was during his slow recovery that he invented his "frequently discussed family life" (X, 421).

These two gentlemen like to play an occasional game of cards with a third, Csemez by name, a professor of chemistry whose eccentricity is to dabble in alchemy hoping to discover a method whereby base metals may be converted into gold. Krisztina, Csemez's nubile daughter, becomes the object of contention between Csutkás and Luppán when, on one occasion, Csutkás proves bold enough to ask for her hand in marriage. While Csemez explains that he is not willing to part with his daughter except to a suitor who is willing to exchange her for her weight in gold, Krisztina departs in bewilderment. Outside, she runs into some friends, a brother and a sister, who happen to be on their way to visit her. Krisztina throws herself into the arms of the brother, Miklós, who is both shocked and delighted by this sudden, unexpected, and impetuous declaration of love. Krisztina is, of course, merely trying to escape the unpleasant possibility of marrying either of her father's friends. Because of Krisztina's confused and erratic behavior, Miklós soon grasps at least part of the truth and elicits from Krisztina a confession that although not " 'in love with another,' " she has a " 'dream of a man' " whose features, as it turns out, are lifted from popular romances, who is, in short, a composite of novelistic heroes (X, 433). Krisztina's Romantic preconditioning continues to play a prominent role in the remainder of the story. When Csemez reasserts that he shall never give his daughter except to a suitor who will exchange her for her weight in gold, Miklós declares with a Romantic flourish that he shall either produce the gold or die in the attempt. Krisztina's response to this novelistic gesture is equally Romantic. The young man has now apparently won her undying love (X, 439).

The conclusion of the story is as ironic as it is swift. Miklós, who has journeyed first to California and then to South America, for long periods of time is seldom heard of. Meanwhile Krisztina's father dies and the entire "gold deal" is really no longer in effect. Krisztina continues to wait for her "hero," and her waiting is frequently punctuated by visits from her former suitors who are now themselves beyond the age of marriage. Years later news reaches Krisztina that Miklós has accumulated as much as half a ton of gold when last seen in Brazil (X, 444). It appears that Krisztina's young man has found happiness in what was once but the means for happiness and that the acquisition of gold has become an end in itself. All this is related in the conclusion to the story in a matter of a page or two. The theme of the irreconcilable conflict between the Romantic and Realistic responses to life's possibilities is played out at the expense of the first. There is, however, no moralizing here. The attempt to model life on Romantic fiction is of the characters' own devising. Krisztina's father, Krisztina, and Miklós are all aware that they are trying to duplicate the Romantic gestures they have picked up from popular novels they read, but they remain unaware of the fact that such gestures lead nowhere in "real" life.

"Az a fekete folt" ("That Black Stain") takes the reader in an apparently different direction. The story appears to be an anti-fairy tale, the idyllic atmosphere of which is stained, or rather, blotted out by an act of desperation. A prince, in proper fairy-tale fashion, falls in love with his shepherd's daughter. The shepherd, however, is unwilling to "sell" her for the sake of his own material advancement. When the prince elopes with the girl, leaving behind the deed to the pastures, the shepherd burns his property and disappears from the region. This is a mature tale in which human motivations, although handled indirectly as is typical of Mikszáth, are presented with the kind of complexity appropriate to the modern novel. The tale is full of portentous echoes of "human lies" (referring to socially accepted formalities) and the unformed thoughts of "primordial poetry" (X, 449, 451). This primordial poetry is pregnant with the notion that human "speech . . . is gospel to those who believe in it" (X, 456). The story's plot is really a structural enactment of this notion. When the prince comes to ask for his daughter's hand in marriage and promises to make a gift to the old man of the lands and sheep in his care, the shepherd is deeply wounded. According to the sense of honor prevalent in the world of primordial poetry in which he dwells, acceptance of the prince's gift would be tantamount to selling his daughter for the sake of his own selfish ends; thus, it would amount to a permanent stain upon his honor.

The prince soon notices that his offer is not going to be accepted. He tries to undo the damage by putting his offer in a different context, one which would keep the old shepherd's honor intact. If he were to elope with the old man's daughter, this would happen without the shepherd's knowledge, thus it would be attributed to the " 'hand of fate' " and no dishonor could possibly accrue to the old man. But the old shepherd knows that this would only save the *appearance* of his honor. Once the prince's offer had been spoken, nothing can unsay it. The old man's response to this suggested solution makes this unmistakably clear: " 'why have you spoken then . . . why haven't you acted instead' " (X, 465). The prince quickly decides to act, but now it is too late. The old man's tacit agreement cancels the element of fate. His honor may be *apparently* saved, but he himself would know better. By the time the shepherd sends word to the prince that the deal is off, however, the prince has already eloped with his daughter. Now the "stain" upon the old man's honor can only be wiped out by the black stain upon the landscape itself, left behind by the burnt land and sheepfold. The invisible or metaphoric stain can only be annihilated by the visible or literal stain which thus becomes the sign or symbol of the father's uncompromising refusal to "sell" his daughter. Thus the subtle clash between appearance and reality is a repetition of the theme of Romanticism vs. Realism but with a difference. Here the Romantic vision of "primordial poetry" triumphs over the Realistic temptation of materialistic self-interest.

The next story in the volume, "Lapaj, a hires dudás" ("Lapaj, the Famous Bagpiper") suggests a similar theme about primordial poetry. It is a sentimental tale about an old, taciturn misanthrope whose heart is softened by a foundling. When his unexpected "fatherhood" requires that he sell his famous bagpipe in order to buy provisions for the baby girl, he is willing to sacrifice one source of joy in his life for another. Again, love kindled by the foundling burns away all materialistic considerations. The final story in the volume, "Jasztrabek pusztulása" ("The Destruction of the Jasztrab Gang"), provides us with an early version of one of Mikszáth's many eccentrics. It is the story of a lawman, István Gerge, who outsmarts the famous Jasztrab gang by using one of its members as his own spy. Because Gerge seems to know everything the members of the gang do, he is soon credited with "omniscience." In the end, when only Jasztrab is still at large, Gerge decides to capture the gang leader himself. Here the lawman gambles with his life on the chance that Jasztrab's bullets will miss him. When the smoke clears from in front of the highwayman's face, Gerge stands there with two bullets in his hands, allowing Jasztrab to think that these are the bullets he had just fired and that Gerge had caught them. The lawman proves himself to be a consummate con man who, by creating the illusion of omniscience and omnipotence, clears up the region under his jurisdiction.

The four stories in *A tót atyafiak* may not be the best their author was to write, but they do provide us with insights into some of Mikszáth's most important themes. The first delineates the detrimental effects of Romantic delusions in the lives of its characters, while the last depicts the beneficial effects of one man's ability to create illusions which are meant to be mistaken for realities. Of the stories in between, "Az a fekete folt" is an especially profound study of the subtle interaction between appearance and reality and how knowing the difference between the two may force an honest man to opt for the preservation of both. Different configurations of these themes will crop up again and again in the works of Mikszáth's maturity, each time with new emphases and with ever wider possibilities of application to the human condition.

IV A jó palócok *(1882)*

If the publication of *A tót atyafiak* had created for Mikszáth a substantial reading public, the appearance of *A jó palócok (The Good Palóc People)* shortly thereafter placed his fame and popularity on a permanent basis. Contemporary reviewers hailed the author of the new volume as the Hungarian Bret Harte (Bret Harte's *The Luck of Roaring Camp and Other Stories* [1870] was well known and highly acclaimed in Hungary at this time),[14] and they stated that the stories in *A jó palócok* are "veritable folk ballads in prose."[15] Mikszáth's indebtedness to folk and fairy tales is perhaps nowhere more apparent than in this volume. One of his critics noted, and rightly so, that the law that governs these tales is the inevitable punishment of evil and the equally inevitable triumph of the good.[16] For the sake of convenience I shall not discuss these stories in the order in which they appear in the volume, but in accordance with four broadly conceived, albeit somewhat arbitrarily chosen, categories. Some of the stories fall into a category of stories about greed and corruption, some into the category of love, licit and illicit, some into that of legal justice vs. moral justice, and, finally, a number of the stories can be grouped under the broad heading of appearance vs. reality. These categories are not clear-cut, and many of the stories in the volume either overlap two or more of them or else defy categorization altogether.

Of the two stories that broadly fit the category of greed and corruption, the first, "A néhai bárány" ("The Late Lamb"), is little more than an anecdote built around the folklorish motif of the greedy, well-to-do man who, to add to his possessions, kills a poor child's pet lamb. The story progresses installment by installment with the kind of indirect narration characteristic of Mikszáth. A remote Catholic village is threatened by heavy rains. The frantic ringing of the church bells seems to drive away the danger, but the little river that runs through the vicinity is swelling with alarming rapidity and brings with it signs of flooding in the regions lying above. At one point a hope chest is seen floating on the river amidst the multitude of debris, and on it sits a little black lamb. As it turns out, the hope chest belongs to a girl in a neighboring village, and its loss represents the loss of her chance for marriage at an early date. The lamb atop the chest is the pet of the girl's younger sister. As the chest floats by the property of the richest man in the village, it mysteriously disappears. The father of the girls tries to recover these lost treasures by having the authorities search the rich man's premises, but this attempt meets with no success. Later the little girl herself confronts the old man in public, demanding the return of her lamb. The embarrassed rich man is about to swear to God that he knows nothing of the animal's disappearance when his coat slips aside and reveals the lamb's fur in its inner lining.

"A kis csizmák" ("The Small Boots"), the second story that fits into this category, is also about human justice on the one hand, and divine justice on the other. It is about a rich man inflicted by serious problems on all sides. His children are sick and dying and his wealth is fast dwindling away. In order to propitiate God, he attempts to invest his remaining fortune in gifts that may be pleasing to the Creator. But the picture of the Virgin he acquires for the local church is lost in an accident, and the cross he erects in a local cemetery is struck by lightning. The rich man's fortune does not turn for the better until, instead of expensive memorials, he buys a pair of small boots for the village orphan.

These stories are characterized by a highly moral tone unrelieved by humor. This is not true of the stories that fit into the category of love, licit and illicit. "A bágyi csoda" ("The Miracle at Bágy"), for example, is more humorous than moralistic although it is a brilliant vignette about illicit love. The miracle at Bágy is really not a miracle at all. Rather, it is the ironic fulfillment of a "prophecy." The miller's wife once remarks that the day she is unfaithful to her husband, the rivulet at Bágy will turn around and flow backward. At the time of the story the miller himself is away in the army. When his wife's former lover gains admittance to her house under the pretext that the night is cold, he tells the millhand to let down the floodgates to prolong the grinding of his wheat. While the former lover thus spends the night with the miller's wife, the waters accumulate around the sluice until finally, unable to flood because of the strong dams, they turn around and flow backward.

"Szegény Gélyi János lovai" ("Poor János Gélyi's Horses") is a sequel to "A bágyi csoda" (although it comes much later in the volume). János Gélyi, the one-time lover of the miller's wife, is now married to her. As he is readying his famous horses for a nearby wedding, he overhears a conversation between his wife and an old woman. The conversation is apparently about a potential meeting between Gélyi's wife and some new lover. On their way to the wedding, having been confirmed by further signs that his wife is unfaithful to him, he drives his horses off a precipice. What was but a bawdy tale while Gélyi was still his present wife's lover now turns into a domestic tragedy. In these stories Mikszáth does not moralize. His authorial intrusions are at a minimum, and they have little to do with the moral implicit in the tales. The moral is evident in the characters' actions. The narrator's tone merely coincides with the attitude of his presumed audience.

The next two stories that fit the category of love, licit and illicit, also sound like folk ballads in prose, but here we also deal with motives suggested by the stories of Tristan and Isolde and Romeo and Juliet. "Két major regénye" ("The Novel of Two Manors") incorporates elements from both. Of two shepherds who hate one another because of past quarrels over the rights to common grazing grounds, the first has a son, the second a daughter. When the story opens the first shepherd's son is dying. His last wish is that his father ask for the daughter of his enemy's hand in marriage. If the answer is in the affirmative, the father is to use a certain set of bells on the returning flock so that the son may hear from afar that his wish has been granted. The two shepherds reconcile with one another and the story is apparently headed for a happy ending when it turns out that the daughter of the second, who has evidently received news of her lover's terminal illness, drowns herself. The sad father returns only to find that his son has also died during that day.

"Timár Zsófi özvegysége" ("Zsófi Timár's Widowhood") also utilizes the Tristan and Isolde motif. This is the story of an abandoned wife who, as the years go by, hopes that her husband will return to her. The people of her village frequently whisper about her apparently vain hope, but one day she does receive news of her repentant husband. As Zsófi (ready to forgive) arrives at the village where her renegade husband has been working, he falls off the church steeple, and this time Zsófi really becomes a widow.

Of the stories in this category "Hova lett Gál Magda?" ("Where Has Magda Gál Gone?") is the best. It is subtly built around a proverb popular in Hungary: the pitcher will continue to go to the well until it breaks. The sense of the proverb is similar to "he who lives by the sword shall die by the sword." The story involves the communal well of a village, horse traders who spend some time in the locality, Magda Gál who falls in love with one of them (a married man), and her mother who insists that Magda's subsequent disappearance is attributable to her own threats about breaking any more pitchers. The narrator knows that Magda's disappearance is not due to the virtue of obedience carried to an extreme, but to the girl's vulnerability to "fall" when sorely tempted. Furthermore, the narrator also knows that Magda's mother does not really believe her own explanation for her daughter's disappearance. It is true that on that fateful evening she does tell Magda not to come home if she breaks another pitcher at the well, but this merely explains the verisimilitude of her otherwise unbelievable explanation. Yet the narrator does not poke fun at her. And neither do her fellow villagers. Everyone (the reader included) seems to understand this defense mechanism of a loving mother's broken heart. In this story Mikszáth is at his best.

Naively conceived, legal justice vs. moral justice may be merely a version of good triumphing over evil. This is not the case in "Bede Anna tartozása" ("Anna Bede's Debt"). As the story opens a young girl appears in front of a row of stern magistrates in answer to a summons to begin a six-month prison term. The girl comes in place of her sister, Anna, who has died recently. As she explains, her sister died deeply repentant, and the girl, in order to assure Anna's peace of mind beyond the grave, wants to make sure that her sister's debt to society will not go unpaid. The magistrates are touched by the girl's naivete and honesty and tell her that Anna has since been proven innocent so that there is no more debt to pay. This spontaneous legal fiction is an ingenious triumph over legality. Since Anna is dead, she can no longer be punished for her crime, but since Anna's sister would not comprehend this, the magistrates officially pretend Anna's innocence not to disturb the integrity of her sister's intended self-sacrifice.

The next story, "A királyné szoknyája" ("The Queen's Skirt"), is not quite so subtle an application of the theme of legal justice vs. moral justice. When their mother dies, Imre and Eszter get two worthless pieces of land (a mountain and a valley) from their stepfather, while their half-sister, Erzsi, gets the fertile land known as the Queen's Skirt. At first the orphans try to fight the unjust settlement with the help of the law, but the law proves adamant. As it turns out, however, the mountain and the valley contain coal and other valuable minerals so that the orphans become rich while the greedy father of their half-sister remains poor.

"Az a pogány Filcsik" ("That Pagan Filcsik") is the first of a series of stories that deal with appearance vs. reality. In the context of the story Filcsik appears to be a hard old man. When his daughter runs off with the judge of a neighboring village because she refuses to marry the lame miller her father had chosen for her, Filcsik denies his daughter. Later, when his daughter is sick and dying and her sole wish is to be reconciled to her father, he still refuses to acknowledge her. The only way the judge can get Filcsik to visit her is by having the old man's fur coat stolen for which, as everyone knows, old Filcsik has an inordinate love. When Filcsik comes to claim his fur coat, he also sees his dying daughter; yet, he remains apparently unmoved and unforgiving. On the way home, however, he uses his beloved fur coat to cover a beggar woman and her sleeping child. Yet, for the rest of his life, his reputation is that of a "pagan" and a "godless, bad Christian" (X, 537, 538).

"Szücs Pali szerencséje" ("Pali Szücs's Luck") is a more subtle configuration of the same theme. Pali Szücs, on his way to ask Erzsi Bede's hand in marriage, finds a four-leaf clover. This sign of good luck does appear to bring its finder precisely that. The young man, who once had a reputation for riotous and irresponsible living, has been diligent for some time now. Furthermore, on his way to the Bede house, he encounters an acquaintance who promises him a lucrative contract. Erzsi's mother is also willing to agree to the alliance now that the bridegroom-to-be is a promising youth. On his way home, however, the lucky Pali Szücs cannot resist the temptation to stop by a local tavern and celebrate his engagement and good fortune. He gets drunk and carouses till the wee hours of the morning. His future employer sees him and decides against the promised contract. By the time Pali is carried home, his engagement kerchief has also been returned. The story ends with Pali's thinking that perhaps he has never been to the Bede house, perhaps he has dreamed the whole affair.

It is clear that Pali Szücs is the victim of self-deception. The four-leaf clover does not bring him luck. His own diligence is responsible for the change in his fortune, even as it is his own falling back to his previous bad habits that undermines it. "A gózoni Szüz Mária" ("The Virgin Mary of Gózon") is also about deception, but here the deception is not self-directed. This is another pseudo-miracle tale built around a love triangle. Gábor Csuz pays court to the charlatan Panna Gughi who is reputed to be the Virgin's favorite. Once, during a pilgrimage, Panna deceives the good folk with many stories in which she supposedly saw the Virgin and had privileged dealings with her. When Panna describes the Virgin, the people believe her since her description fits the conventional representations of the madonna in prayer books and on the walls of churches. On the night of the pilgrimage Gábor has an illicit meeting with Panna at the place where the Virgin had supposedly appeared to the girl in times past. This time a madonna-like figure with a babe does come upon the scene, but it is not the Virgin; rather, it is Gábor's seduced and abandoned sweetheart from a neighboring village. The story ends with the guilt-ridden Panna's mistaking this unwed mother for the Mother of God. As is customary with all the stories in *A jó palócok*, the "Gózoni Szüz" ends abruptly.

Panna is a deliberate deceiver, momentarily deceived by her own conscience. In the case of old Filcsik, his fellow villagers deceive themselves about him and the old man is indifferent to their deception. Pali Szücs, on the other hand, deceives himself by refusing to recognize that he could be the master of his own fate. These facts are revealed about these characters in action, not by the narrator's moralizing, even though the narrator's moral outlook is crucial to these stories. But this moral outlook is not didactic; it is not interested in teaching the reader how to act or what to avoid; rather, it is interested in sharing with the reader stories that reflect the deepest sense of his own humanity. As one of Mikszáth's critics has noted, the authorial attitude in these stories coincides with the attitude of the village folk.[17] But, as another critic has rightly pointed out, Mikszáth writes about the local *sub specie aeternitatis.*[18] What characterizes the stories in *A jó palócok* is a subtle combination of these two attitudes. In this sense the attitude of the village folk emerges as the pinnacle on the vantage point of eternity. Truth is both local and relative in that each case is unique and must be judged on its own level and in its own terms: and it is universal and absolute in that once its own level and its own terms have been delineated, it spontaneously fits into a whole that transcends truth paradoxically by being firmly rooted in its particular manifestations.

The coincidence between the attitude of the author and that of the village folk on the one hand, and the attitude of the narrator and that of the reader on the other, is further enhanced by the fact that the same characters keep showing up in different stories. The protagonist in one will be a mere "extra" in another, and *vice versa*. This lends a unity and a sense of continuity to the volume which is not unlike the unity of James Joyce's *Dubliners* or the continuity of Sherwood Anderson's *Winesburg, Ohio*.

V *Short Masterpieces*

The two stories discussed in this section are meant to be examples of a relatively large number of shorter works (these are usually longer than short stories and shorter than short novels) that Mikszáth wrote. "Galamb a kalitkában" ("Dove in a Cage"; 1891) is a particularly interesting example of Mikszáth's contribution to this genre. The theme of the story is quite explicitly literature itself, or more precisely the changing mode of literary perception of reality. It is actually two stories in one, or one story narrated twice. The subtitle of the original publication, "Romanticism and Realism," is the first clue to its meaning. "The First Narrative" sounds like a tale out of Boccaccio. It chronicles the fate of two amateur botanists, their love for the same girl, and their incredibly generous friendship, a friendship that is willing to push each of the friends to the point of the utmost personal self-sacrifice. "The Second Narrative" is an up-to-date version of the same story. It is the story of two politicians, their love for the same girl, and their selfishness or unwillingness to sacrifice any sort of comfort or gain for each other's sake.

In the brief "Preface to the Two Narratives" there is a further clue to Mikszáth's playing with the changing mode of literary perception. In it the "author" informs his readers that the "muse," now an "aging lady," had long ago dismissed "fantasy," her "beautiful chambermaid," and had hired instead a "morose jack-of-all-trades: observation" (VII, 355). The whole story, then, is a humorously serious study of what is observable in the world of fantasy and of what is fantastic in the realm of observation.

"The First Narrative" takes the reader four hundred years into the past, to Renaissance Italy. Baduin of Verona decides to pay a visit to his famous fellow botanist, Albertus of Naples. The admitted passion of both men is to cultivate rare roses. Shortly after the arrival of his friend, Albertus tells Baduin that when ready to return home, he may take with him a cutting from any of Albertus's famous roses. Baduin soon notices that there is a secret place in a remote section of Albertus's garden, an arbor-like summerhouse entwined by climbers. When inquiring about this " 'cage-like' " house, Baduin is told that it holds a " 'secret,' " that there is a " 'dove' " encaged in it (VII, 358). This does not satisfy his curiosity. Upon further inquiries, this time from Albertus's gardener, Baduin is told that the " 'cage' " holds a " 'rose' " (VII, 359). Thinking that his friend has tried to keep his most precious possession a secret, Baduin decides to leave Naples. Albertus learns why his friend has a sudden wish to depart, and, in an attempt to show that his friendship knows no bounds, decides to make a gift to Baduin of the "rose" in the "cage." This turns out to be a beautiful maid whom Albertus had intended to marry at the right time. Baduin does not wish to accept this gift (although he is instantly smitten by the girl's beauty), but when Estre herself indicates that she desires to live with Baduin, the deal is made.

The heartbroken Albertus then sells his property and decides to travel far and wide in a desperate attempt to forget his "dove." He quickly spends his fortune (a highwayman helps him to get rid of some of it, too) and years later arrives in Verona little more than a beggar. Here, planning to visit Baduin, and hoping to receive pity and assistance from his old friend, Albertus spends the night in an empty funeral parlor adjacent to a cemetery. In the middle of the night a commotion awakens him. A murder has just been committed nearby, and every circumstance points to Albertus as the guilty party. The judge does not believe Albertus's story (twice he refers to it as a "fairy tale," VII, 368), and the "vagabond" is finally condemned to die. Just as the execution is about to be carried out, Baduin comes forth to confess to the murder. Then the real murderer, moved by the self-abnegating act of friendship he has just witnessed, himself confesses. The judge, in turn, decides to spare the real murderer's life since " 'he has loved justice more than his life' " (VII, 376). Now "The First Narrative" quickly comes to a conclusion. Baduin informs Albertus that Estre is still a maid. Since she really loved Albertus all along, Baduin has merely watched over her until such time as her true love may return and claim her. Baduin has also invested Estre's dowry wisely so that Albertus will once again be a rich man.

Such is the first story, but its final words are not its own. Just as he is about to conclude, the narrator is interrupted by outraged imaginary readers who find the story utterly incredible. The narrator seems to listen calmly to the harangue of one implied reader who claims that these characters could never possibly have existed since they all " 'suffer from an excess of goodness.' " After a while the narrator seems to lose his patience, too, at which point it is his turn to interrupt the reader and exclaim that "there is nothing wrong with these characters . . . but that they lived four hundred years ago" (VII, 379).

"The Second Narrative" takes the reader to "present-day" Budapest. István Altorjay, a politician, is about to marry Eszter Willner, a young lady with a generous dowry. His friend, Péter Korláthy, another politician, is to be the best man. On the eve of the wedding, however, Péter elopes with Eszter. When the happy couple returns to Budapest, Péter challenges István to a duel because the latter had made a disparaging remark about the character of the former. After the duel (where István receives a slight wound) the "friends" achieve a reconciliation. When Eszter's dowry runs out, Péter makes an offer of her to István. According to his own interpretation, Péter does this because he is prompted by his own sense of " 'honesty.' " Now that the dowry is spent, however, István does not wish to be " 'saddled' " with the " 'mere woman' " (VII, 404). Since he cannot get rid of his now unwanted wife, Péter goes abroad. After a while his wife decides to follow him. But first she needs money which she obtains by cashing a forged check. In Hamburg (where, it is implied, she lives as a prostitute for a while) she eventually runs into her husband who is apparently traveling with an aging but wealthy American lady. Péter, knowing that his wife is wanted by the Hungarian police for forgery, secretly informs the authorities of Eszter's whereabouts. As the story ends Eszter is in jail, Péter, living happily with his "English person," is heading some sort of honors committee, and István is still a politician (VII, 418).

The final words of "The Second Narrative" are also taken up by the "author" himself. Why has he written this story at all, he asks. "I don't know," he informs us, "but I regret [having written] it already. Perhaps I wanted to poke fun at ancient writers, ancient readers, and ancient books, and by doing so show our own in a favorable light." This statement provokes a further dialogue between the "author" and his "readers." An implied reader states that the two stories are not really comparisons between two ages, that they are both nothing but " 'ink.' " Then the so-called "general reader" interjects that " 'stories do not change, only people do.' " The "wise shake their heads" at this. According to them it is " 'precisely people who do not change, only stories do.' " By this time the "critics" are said to be rather "nervous." They explain that " 'neither stories, nor people change, only literary fashions.' " Hearing these "sound" arguments, the "author" simply decides to stop writing, that is, to end this particular story (VII, 419–20).

What is, of course, implicit in the story as a whole is that none of these arguments is adequate. If the "fantasy" that, according to the "Preface," produces "The First Narrative" is hopelessly guided by idealism ("Romanticism" in terms of the story's original subtitle), the observation that produces the second is equally hopelessly guided by cynicism ("Realism" as the subtitle has it). The point of the story is quite clearly that neither "fantasy" nor "observation" can operate with objectivity, or, better, with innocence. The undiscussed assumption underlying each colors what each paints. Perhaps the fact that the modern reader finds "The Second Narrative" credible is itself a judgment on the modern reader.

"A gavallérok" ("The Big Spenders"; 1897) also pits a kind of naivete (this time the narrator's) against a kind of cynicism (the reader's), but here the story itself seems to turn the tables on both. In the end both the "author" and his "readers" gain a kind of compassion for the "big spenders" who turn out to be self-conscious "fakes." In comparison with most of Mikszáth's stories, "A gavallérok" is practically plotless. It is basically the description of an expensive wedding in Northeastern Hungary as recounted by a newspaperman from Budapest who happens to be the bridegroom's friend. In the beginning the narrator makes much of the fact that the bridegroom, being a poor journalist himself, could use a substantial dowry. What he sees as he witnesses the preparations for the wedding seems to indicate that this is precisely what the bridegroom will receive. The whole countryside seems to be up and about, and the very richest men of the region all seem to be members of the wedding. Fancy carriages drawn by four horses each seem to be legion, as well as liveried servants. The narrator runs into rich foods and expensive wines everywhere. At the wedding itself the bride's father makes a touching speech as he turns over to the new couple a check made out to the sum of fifty thousand forints. The bridegroom's father, not wanting to be outdone by his new in-law, presents the happy couple with a check worth sixty thousand forints. The members of the wedding receive each of these generous gestures with deafening applause and roof-raising shouts of joy, and the narrator himself is amazed and happy for his "former" colleague.

Although there are a number of clues to the contrary (at a card game, for example, the losers seem to be cheerful while the winners seem to remain perversely indifferent), the narrator never suspects that what he sees is not what is. When the wedding guests depart in the heavy fog of the morning, the narrator gets a ride to the nearest town in one of the many fancy carriages. As the fog lifts, so does the narrator's ignorance. At the point of departure each carriage is drawn by four horses and each is occupied by no more than two or three guests. As the carriages progress through the countryside, the number of horses also diminishes. Soon each of the remaining carriages has many occupants huddling together in the cold morning air and each is drawn by one horse, perhaps two. The implication becomes unmistakable. As the narrator's partner informs him, " 'nothing here is what it appears to be' " (VIII, 93). And everything turns out to have been rented or borrowed. Even the checks the new couple received turn out to have been fakes. When the narrator exclaims, " 'but this is downright deception.' " his partner's response is " 'balderdash . . . everyone knows of everyone else that they don't own four horses. These good fellows are merely keeping up appearances . . . and it's such a pleasure. What harm can you possibly see in it?' " But the narrator is still puzzled. If everyone knows that nothing is real, why are they all so happy, why do they applaud and cheer empty gestures? His partner gives further testimony: " 'we are constantly holding dress rehearsals of how we would act were we to become rich. And when the show is a success, we are glad, we applaud ourselves. And when we see that a stranger takes it all for real, *we know for sure that we have acted flawlessly* . . . and as far as the valuables are concerned, they, too, belong to somebody, if not to one, then to another . . . [and] the pomp, the radiance . . . the sophistication . . . belong to us all. It's just that everything is well distributed and dispersed, but if on occasion we artificially bring it all together, who is to say whether it's true or not?' " (VIII, 97, italics Mikszáth's).

By the end of this story what appeared to be real but turned out to be fake appears to be more real than if it had been real in the first place. In this sense "A gavallérok" is one of fiction's warmest, most compassionate triumphs over drab reality. And the fact that it uses a naive narrator who turns cynical before he is finally enlightened enhances this effect for the reader precisely because even as the narrator comes to see the light, so does the reader. The revelation at the end of the story, then, is almost a religious one. It is almost as though the human spirit itself took collective charge of its illusions and invested them with reality, as on a holiday, while it never lost sight of them as illusions of its own making. Mikszáth's art in this story is such that the reader's initial disappointment at realizing that nothing is what it seems to be is quickly transformed into a gaiety which insists that everything that seems to be, after all, is.

This brief examination of the shorter works reveals not only Mikszáth's evolving artistry but also his most characteristic thematic preoccupations. These usually incorporate either a conflict between the Romantic and the Realistic, or a clash between appearance and reality. But the relationship between these similar themes is not necessarily inversely proportionate. That is to say, the Romantic is not necessarily a rejection of "mere" appearances, and the Realistic is not necessarily a recommendation of the way things are. Mikszáth's novels will continue to show ever more complex configurations of these basic themes. The particular pros and cons of Romanticism and Realism, or of appearance and reality, will continually battle with one another for supremacy. Each case will make it clear, however, just why and in what sense the reader should accept the one or the other as the victorious principle. It will soon be apparent that from a thematic point of view Mikszáth's novels are not appreciably different from his shorter works. Their overall effect, however, is highly cumulative. It is as though with each additional novel the reader were approaching the privileged position of viewing a basic set of human problems from an infinite number of ever more illuminating and ever more penetrating points of view.

CHAPTER 3

The Early Novels

I Beszterce ostroma *(1894)*

Beszterce ostroma (The Siege of Beszterce), written in forty-seven serial installments, first appeared in book form in 1896 with the subtitle: "The Story of an Eccentric." It is essentially the story of a mad nobleman who imagines himself to be a great medieval lord and who is powerful enough to actually enact this role. The first half of the narrative is a chronicle of Count István Pongrácz's motive for attempting to besiege the town of Beszterce. The immediate background of the aborted siege is the elopement of Estella (whom the Count looks upon as his own personal property) with a young nobleman, a member of Pongrácz's retinue. When the authorities of Beszterce refuse even to consider giving up the renegades, the Count decides to raze the city. In order to save Pongrácz from the scandal the siege would bring in its wake, his friends and relatives divert him from his intention by hiring a group of actors who "represent" the town of Beszterce. The "delegation" brings a hostage to the Count in the person of Apollonia, an orphan whom the mayor of the city of Zsolna is eager to place with a respectable family.

Pongrácz is satisfied with the performance and decides to have mercy on Beszterce. The second half of the narrative is a chronicle of the Count's aborted plans for Apollonia whom he learns to love with a kind of religious reverence. Just as the Count is preparing to officially adopt his new charge, a young man from Apollonia's past comes back into her life to claim her hand in marriage. The Count's plans, of course, are in radical opposition to the young couple's nuptials. The bridegroom-to-be's only recourse is to find Estella and exchange her for the Count's "hostage." Pongrácz's sense of honor does not permit him to counter this move, so the mad nobleman decides to commit suicide because (as it is clear by this time in the novel) without Apollonia he has nothing to live for.

This basic plot, which is subtly complicated in its unfolding, actually amounts to what most of Mikszáth's critics have called the Hungarian Quixote.[1] But the connection between Cervantes's masterpiece and Mikszáth's own novel requires more than a mere mention of its existence, and previous critics have not taken advantage of it as a key with which to unlock the metafictional theme explicitly present in *Beszterce ostroma.* As I shall repeatedly have occasion to emphasize, the theme of fiction, the theme of self-generated illusions, is one of Mikszáth's favorite preoccupations. And this theme usually functions as an exposure of societal fictions, as an exposure of the countless illusions various and sundry classes are wont to weave around themselves either for gain or for protection against an otherwise unbearable reality. Many of Mikszáth's characters are more or less self-conscious fiction makers, and Mikszáth seems to have a special liking for those among them who are guided by high ideals, who—like Count Pongrácz—almost believe in the reality of their own fictions, precisely because their own fictions are in some sense grander, more glorious than the fictions of those around them.

The "Preface" to the novel is itself not just an account of the provenance of the story but a clue to its metafictional theme. The "author" (Mikszáth seems to speak in his own person here, but it becomes clear that this is a pose) recalls numerous conversations in a café with the still living relatives of Count István Pongrácz. At first these conversations are merely amusing; soon, however, the "author" realizes that his attitude as listener has changed, that he has become interested in carving a narrative out of the reminiscences of the Count's relatives. Before proceeding with this enterprise, however, he feels it necessary to obtain permission to write the Count's story. When the author considers the propriety of using some fictitious name in lieu of the hero's real name, one of the Count's relatives urges the author to " 'let [the story] use [the hero's] own proper name. If he were to rise from his grave, he would be the happiest at seeing it in print. Anyway, I think that on occasion he himself has desired some such thing' " (I, 382).

Mikszáth gives us a true account of the provenance of the story in his "Open Letter to Miklós Nagy, Editor of the *Vasárnapi Ujság*" (*Sunday Journal*, I, 569–72). From this letter we learn that

Beszterce ostroma is based on fact, and also that Mikszáth has apparently been accused by some of his contemporaries of having been rather free with his treatment of the "facts."[2] In his defense Mikszáth resorts to an ingeniously tongue-in-cheek fiction in which he claims to have heard from Armand himself that his story *(Camille)* as recorded by Alexandre Dumas, Fils is an unacceptable distortion of what *really* happened. What Mikszáth implies here implicitly is that different narrators see things from different points of view and that different points of view necessarily present different versions of the same core reality. To this Mikszáth adds the statement that in the final analysis "what is not credible in *Beszterce ostroma* is factual, what is credible in it is my own invention, that is, that which has never happened." What is Mikszáth's own invention in the story is the theatrical performance with which his friends and relatives persuade Pongrácz not to besiege Beszterce and the whole story of Apollonia together with the Count's fatherly relationship to her.

At the time the narrative commences, Count Pongrácz runs his castle (really an ancient fortress which the Austro-Hungarian authorities permit to be reclassified as "castle" lest, according to law, it be destroyed) in accordance with the rules and regulations of constant medieval warfare. He fights mock battles with a retired officer, and at the end of these battles (regardless of their outcome) he holds grand celebrations. Since there is no "lady" in Nedec Castle, the Count's guests usually come without their respective wives. To remedy this impropriety, the Count "purchases" a young acrobat (Donna Estella by stage name) for six hundred forints (I, 387). Estella soon becomes a fixture at Nedec, and, although she receives frequent beatings, she plays her role well in accordance with the proprieties belonging to a medieval "lady," especially at the many tournaments which the Count holds and which are duly recorded by his scribe.

Estella acts as though she were in love with the Count, thinking it entirely possible for her eccentric "owner" to eventually marry her. According to the narrator, though, the likelihood of this remains in doubt since the Count seems to regard Estella more as a pet than as a woman. At this point the narrator raises the issue of the Count's sanity. His theory is that had the Count not inherited a fortress, he would probably have become a doctor or a lawyer. As he had inherited a fortress (and the rank and name to go with it), he seems to have decided to outwit the inevitable ravages of time by living in accordance with a former age since being the "last suzerain lord" is more to his liking than his nineteenth-century status would be. Here the narrator mischievously remarks that it is not *his* business to speculate about such matters anyway. His business is to write about the "affairs of István Pongrácz, as they really happened" (I, 392).

The Count is altogether dissatisfied with the present and with its inhabitants. The best indication of this is that instead of a real woman, he chooses to love the portrait of a grand lady long dead. In time even his retinue seems to turn a bit crazy, almost coming to believe that they are indeed the servants of some great medieval lord. Perhaps nothing would interrupt this serene obsolescence were it not for a nobleman in the neighborhood whose son, Baron Károly Behenczy, a semi-impoverished confidence man, decides to join the retinue at Nedec Castle. As a number of other characters in the story, Behenczy, too, is willing to humor the Count and is self-consciously acting a part. On arriving, for example, he makes a formal bow and declares that he has come to Nedec to "make his fortune" alongside the great count (I, 400). Since Behenzcy claims to have once studied medicine, the Count takes him on as his official "foretaster" (I, 405). Behenczy's wit makes him a favorite with the Count when the young man explains that the eccentric Pongrácz cannot possibly be mad since he knows how to count backward.

Just as the Count is preparing for another "war" (this time with the troops of the real army whose officers think this is an inexpensive way of conducting military exercises), Pongrácz receives a copy of Cervantes's *Don Quixote*, the reading of which seems to have a profound effect upon him. The immediate result of reading this book is the Count's decision to give up his mock wars. With this ploy Mikszáth forces the reader to realize that Count István Pongrácz is a kind of Don Quixote, too. Shortly after Pongrácz's sobering reading of *Don Quixote*, however, Behenczy makes improper advances toward Estella. This act of disloyalty enrages the Count who imprisons the young man in the dungeon and even contemplates his execution. Estella thinks that the Count's harsh judgment is motivated by jealousy. When she learns the contrary, her opportunistic mind forces her to settle for the title of baronness which she hopes to obtain by helping Behenczy escape. Behenczy, fearing for his life, does promise to marry her.

At this point the narrator launches into another series of speculations concerning his hero's sanity. Here, however, his ploy is to question our ability to judge another mind with any degree of certitude. Since we tend to judge with difficulty even the things that are external, immediately apprehensible, how much more difficult it must be to judge accurately the workings of another mind, the effects of which are but partial manifestations of a probably more coherent whole than meets the eye. The only thing, the narrator concludes, we can know with any degree of certainty concerning Pongrácz is that he was "born too late" (I, 419).

When Estella's perfidy is revealed (she helps Behenczy escape by disguising herself as a peasant woman and carrying the Baron on her back in a potato sack), the Count exclaims that the girl has committed a twofold crime in that she has helped the prisoner escape and that she herself has escaped (Estella having been "bought" is, according to the Count, his own personal property). At this point, apparently having completely forgotten the sobering effects of Don Quixote, the Count orders his scribe to write a letter to the appropriate authorities of Beszterce (where Behenczy is said to reside with Estella), demanding the prompt return of his "property," else he will be obliged to wipe the whole town off the face of the earth (I, 423–24). With this letter (which is composed in an archaic style and is modeled on a family heirloom that dates back to the Middle Ages) Pongrácz resumes his role as the "last suzerain lord." But we should keep in mind that from his point of view he is forced to act this way first because of Behenczy's act of disloyalty and then because of Estella's double perfidy. When the town's authorities send a contemptuous reply, Count István Pongrácz decides to reenlist his men and besiege Beszterce.

The second part of the book, the story of Apollonia, details a complicated subplot (not without a great deal of satiric value in its own right) which Mikszáth ingeniously coalesces with the main plot of his novel. The story involves three brothers, the daughter of one and the son of another, and a brother-in-law. This part of *Beszterce ostroma* reads very much like an aborted fairy tale. Two of the brothers decide to go into business; the third decides to become a doctor. The businessmen both prosper; the doctor does not (which was not at all unlikely in nineteenth-century Hungary). When the poverty-stricken doctor dies, his daughter, Apollonia, is up for adoption. The newly orphaned girl becomes the object of contention between the prosperous brothers who, needless to say, hate one another. Their rivalry gets so vicious that the authorities give the girl to a third party, a brother-in-law (whose wife was related to Apollonia's late mother), a poor but apparently kind administrator in the town of Zsolna. At this point the prosperous brothers both refuse to give financial assistance to their brother-in-law; each seems satisfied that his rival did not get the girl. The brother-in-law is somewhat unhappy with this situation since his own motive, as it turns out, in adopting the girl was one of greed. Later the rivalry between the prosperous brothers revives so that eventually a new arrangement is provided for by the authorities: each of the prosperous brothers will keep the girl for six months at a time. This time they try to outdo one another by showering riches upon the girl, and they even go so far as to make a political issue out of the new arrangement. Being of Slovak origin, one of the brothers tries to Hungarianize Apollonia just to provoke the other.

Notwithstanding this constant rivalry, things go relatively well for Apollonia till Miloszláv, the son of one of the brothers, falls in love with her. Once again, both the prosperous brothers reject her. When her former guardian becomes a widower, he promises to "give [Apollonia] a name" (I, 461). This means, of course, marriage between the old man and the very young girl, and this horrifies Apollonia to the point where she attempts suicide. The Mayor of Zsolna finds Apollonia by a river. He is touched by her story and decides to find a respectable family willing to adopt her. At this point Count Pongrácz arrives in Zsolna (which is half-way between Nedec and Beszterce); Apollonia's story will soon blend in with the major plot of the novel.

As the third part of the book opens, Pongrácz is seen arriving at Zsolna. When some of his friends and relatives see Pongrácz with his army and find out what he is up to, they try to humor him, but they also try to dissuade him from besieging Beszterce for fear that were he to do so, the authorities would certainly have him committed. When their pleas that the likes of Estella are not worth the bloodshed and destruction the coming battle would surely bring in its wake prove ineffective, Pongrácz's friends resort to a grand scheme in which Apollonia will figure prominently. First they have to persuade the Mayor of Zsolna that Apollonia will find an excellent guardian in the person of the Count who, according to them, is really not mad. As they put it, the Count's " 'mind is [merely] impregnated with the life-style and glory of his ancestors. Illusions reign in it' " (I, 475). Since this is the case, they decide to "speak to him *in his own language*" by hiring some actors from a nearby theatrical troup who will pretend to be a delegation from Beszterce (I, 476, italics are Mikszáth's). The delegation will come to beg the Count's pardon, and, since Estella has apparently disappeared, they will also beg the count to take Apollonia as a hostage until such time as Estella can be located and returned to her proper "owner."

This plot provides us with another interesting comparison between *Don Quixote* and *Beszterce ostroma*. In *Don Quixote*, too, an attempt is made to enter into the knight's illusion (by Sanson Carrasco who, on two separate occasions, dresses up as a knight to challenge the Don), but here, as Richard L. Predmore has so convincingly shown, the intention is to destroy the illusion by addressing it in its own language.[3] In Mikszáth's novel the friends of the "mad" count are truly interested both in saving him from the insane asylum and in protecting his illusions. The encounter between the Count and the "delegation from Beszterce" is thus not only a highly amusing but also a highly significant one.

Part of the amusement is provided by the fact that the whole performance is in a sense a parody of Chief Árpád's conquest of Hungary. As legend has it, when Árpád penetrated the Carpathian Basin with his seven Hungarian tribes, he asked King Svatopluk to exchange a horse for a bit of water, grass, and earth. The water, grass, and earth were, of course, symbolic of the entire Carpathian Basin; thus King Svatopluk, by granting Árpád's apparently fanciful wish, had actually bartered away a whole kingdom. Part of the ceremony the "delegation from Beszterce" enacts for the Count is the offer of a bit of water, grass, and earth. The Count is pleased with the entire ceremony, for, as the narrator tells us, "his soul, which bathed in the memory of the Middle Ages, was intoxicated even by this glaringly clumsy picture of it. Amidst the illusions in which he had lived since his youth, this was the first reality. Yes, this great lie [was reality itself]" (I, 484).

Apollonia's presence at Nedec Castle works tremendous changes in Count Pongrácz. The old man treats her with religious reverence. He hires companions for her, and, as she grows older and ever more beautiful, her origins become completely obscure: "half the truth was lost in fog, and half in idle rumors. She became a veritable myth" (I, 494). Young men throng to Nedec, each hoping to win

Apollonia. The Count, however, guards her with jealousy. On one occasion he even gets seriously wounded in trying to defend her honor. At this point Apollonia, misguided by the memory of the protective jealousy of a former guardian, thinks that Pongrácz's intentions are also matrimonial. As the Count recuperates, the girl tends to him selflessly in spite of her mounting apprehension that once well the old man will want to marry her. Mikszáth handles this misunderstanding with delicate humor and irony. At one point the Count informs Apollonia that he has no intentions of dying since now he has something to live for. Mikszáth's treatment of Pongrácz is as religiously reverent here as is the Count's treatment of Apollonia. At this point Mikszáth even allows the Count to betray his awareness of his illusions when he has Pongrácz state: " 'I have dreamed about some happiness and now I am confusing it with reality' " (I, 500).

Upon the Count's recovery, Apollonia's misunderstanding is allowed to deepen before it is finally cleared up under highly complicated circumstances. Miloszláv, who has since become a lawyer (and who has changed his name to Emil), is called in to draft a petition to the King for Apollonia's formal adoption. The petition to the King is necessary since this adoption would make Apollonia a countess as well as the official heir of Nedec Castle. When Miloszláv asks for Apollonia's hand in marriage, the Count is once again enraged, and the youth—just as his predecessor—is thrown into the dungeon.

Here the narrator gives us a flashback to a time shortly before the events described above. This information throws significant light on Emil-Miloszláv's character. When Emil's uncle was about to make Apollonia the heir of his fortune, Emil tried to intercept his uncle's intention for fear that were Apollonia to become rich, the world would think that he sought her hand in marriage because of her money. Whatever we may think of this scheme, Mikszáth intends for us to see that the honorable madness from which Pongrácz is suffering can affect others as well.

In the fourth part of the novel, Emil, who finally escapes from the dungeon of Nedec Castle (after the innumerable attempts of the bureaucratic powers fail to obtain his release), begins to renew the old plot "against" the Count with the cooperation of the Mayor of Zsolna. First they "repurchase" Estella from Behenczy (who has, after all, refused to marry her), then they "rehire" the "delegation from Beszterce" who will return with Estella to exchange her for the hostage, Apollonia. When the Count hears of this plot he realizes, like Don Quixote, that his own code of honor forces him to release his charge. Unlike Don Quixote, however, Pongrácz does not die disabused of his illusions. Once the fate of Apollonia, with which of course he has intricately fused his own, is beyond his control, he calmly proceeds to arrange for his own death and funeral. He orders a gigantic coffin to be built since, in accordance with the rites of pagan Huns, he wishes to be buried atop his favorite horse. Then he travels far and wide to say farewell to his relatives and friends, and finally, apparently having poisoned himself, he expires just as the "delegation from Beszterce" is arriving with Estella. His wish to be buried atop his favorite horse is, of course, never fulfilled. Once dead, the Count can no longer forge his own destiny in accordance with his illusions. The Count's unfulfilled wish becomes symbolic of the fact that with his death a certain nobility has disappeared from the face of the earth, never to return. Just before saying "farewell to [his] readers," the narrator once again raises the issue of his hero's sanity, this time to waive his interest in the whole question: "was he really mad, or did he merely pretend to be mad, I myself have no desire to know" (I, 565).

Although the novel consists of four parts (respectively entitled "Estella," "Joyous Offspring," "The Hostage," and "The Night"), the plot is constructed according to two basic movements. A careful look at this plot construction will reveal how attentively Mikszáth embodied a latent meaning in the basic structure of his novel. The center of attention in the first movement (which carries the plot to the performance of the "delegation from Beszterce") is Pongrácz's sense of honor. The interpersonal relations that exist between Pongrácz and Estella, Pongrácz and Behenczy, and Estella and Behenczy represent a maze of cross-purposes, all of which are ultimately strictly "official" or, at best, opportunistic. Pongrácz needs Estella simply because Nedec needs the presence of a "lady," and he tolerates Behenczy simply because the latter fits well into his imaginary world as the "last suzerain lord." Estella wants Behenczy simply because, having failed to become a countess, the role of the baronness offers itself as adequate compensation, and Behenczy needs Estella first because he fears for his life and secondly because she is attractive enough to be a potential gratifier of his lust (although Mikszáth leaves this last item up to the reader's imagination, it is clear that during the long period of their cohabitation Behenczy and Estella have some sexual relations).

In the first movement of the plot Pongrácz's relapse into Quixotism is clearly founded upon one thing and one thing alone: the slur upon his honor. Behenczy's disloyalty, Estella's double perfidy, and Beszterce's aspersive response to the Count's demands are all examples of this. It is the desire to redress the aspersions upon his honor that motivates Pongrácz's attempt to besiege Beszterce, and it is the theatrical satisfaction provided for the Count that diverts his initial vengeful intent.

It is interesting to note that the second movement of the plot utilizes a basic structure which is identical to the first. Here, too, the emphasis is on a triangular relationship that involves Pongrácz and Apollonia on the one hand, and Apollonia and Emil on the other. But here the center of attention shifts from Pongrácz's sense of honor to his sense of religious reverence for Apollonia. Where Estella remains a piece of property, Apollonia clearly becomes a surrogate daughter. Where Behenczy's advances toward Estella are clearly dishonorable, Emil's advances toward Apollonia are motivated by even more honorable intentions than is customary (as witness his desperate attempts not even to want to *seem* to be after her wealth).

Notwithstanding its identical structure, then, this movement is radically different from the first. Where in the first movement Pongrácz attempts to battle for his honor, here he tries desperately to defend his newfound happiness, the only true happiness in his otherwise barren, illusion-filled life. Although his religious reverence for Apollonia is the reverence of a potentially doting father, Pongrácz's "madness" takes on a new dimension when we recognize that his love for Apollonia is as authentic as it is all-consuming. It is, I think, to Pongrácz's credit that when his newfound happiness clashes with his sense of honor, the battle between these two basic impulses in his psyche remains unresolved and unresolvable. Pongrácz's suicide is, in this sense, his sole means of maintaining his illusions while at the same time dispensing with them.

The latent meaning inherent in the structure of the entire novel is at once ironic and profound. It is ironic because it implies that to be honorable is to be mad while to be authentically loving *and* honorable is to be madder still. And it is profound because it implies that total honor and acceptable self-interest are ultimately incompatible with life in the modern world. As a recent critic sees it, what the "shallow, farcical rivalry" between Apollonia's uncles reveals is that these representatives of the bourgeoisie "are just as anachronistic and burdened as Pongrácz, but without the latter's paradoxical greatness."[4] It is the tragic vicissitudes of this paradoxical greatness that Mikszáth's art delineates in *Beszterce ostroma,* and it is the inevitable Quixotism which results that shows up the world of Mikszáth's contemporaries for what it is: reality's barren stage that will no longer bear within its artificial props and scaffoldings the truly highminded, the ideal, and the noble.

II Szent Péter esernyöje *(1895)*

Written in thirty-three installments in the same year it appeared in book form, *Szent Péter esernyöje (St. Peter's Umbrella)* is one of Mikszáth's most popular novels. It exists in English, although it is not at this time readily available.[5] Like *Beszterce ostroma,* this novel also involves an eventually coalescing double plot, but here the transitions between the various plots are as significant as they are intricate, and it is to Mikszáth's credit that the miraculous, supernatural-seeming legend (the first part of the novel is simply called "The Legend") is allowed to precede the realistic and completely rational explanation. By means of this structuring device Mikszáth can also show that natural explanations are never quite adequate in ousting their paradoxically more plausible supernatural counterparts.

The novel is essentially the story of an orphan girl, Veronika, and György (Gyuri) Wibra, the illegitimate son of Pál Gregorics, a wealthy misanthrope. When a weatherbeaten umbrella is placed above the sleeping orphan in a remote Slovak village by an unknown hand, the umbrella changes Veronika's fortune. The parish of the young impoverished priest (Veronika's brother) endows the umbrella with a supernatural origin (St. Peter is said to have placed it above the sleeping child for protection). By this means the small, God-forsaken village of Glogova becomes an important religious shrine and tourist attraction to the lasting enrichment both of its priest and, indirectly, of its inhabitants. The "true" story of the umbrella is, of course, much more complicated than this.

The remainder of the novel is both an account of the true story of the umbrella and of the fortunate joining of the two threads of the story. The misanthropic Pál Gregorics, in an attempt to outwit his greedy relations, as well as in an attempt to insure the present safety and future wealth of his illegitimate son, gradually sells all his property and hoards his money inside the hollowed handle of his umbrella. When he dies without an opportunity to reveal to his son the whereabouts of the fortune, the mystery that has already surrounded his wealth in his lifetime deepens. The greedy relations know that Pál Gregorics has more money than his will indicates, but they are unable to locate it.

Gyuri Wibra, who grows up to become an eminent lawyer, is also tempted by the ever present mirage of his fortune. The last sections of the novel chronicle Gyuri's obsessive search for his phantom wealth and of his gradual and painstaking discovery of the umbrella's mystery. His frantic pursuit of the umbrella takes him to the remote Slovak village where a conflict develops between his desire for his rightful inheritance and his newly inspired love for Veronika. This conflict between wealth and love holds the young man's self-esteem in precarious balance for a while, but the final nonexistence of his inheritance helps him come to terms with love as a more deserving fortune than money.

In terms of its plot construction and general atmosphere, *Szent Péter esernyöje* is very much like a folk or fairy tale. In terms of the way in which Mikszáth handles the provenance and perpetuation of the "legend" of St. Peter's umbrella, however, the novel is also a carefully emplotted exposé of the birth of myth and of the "reality" of the fiction the myth creates. The initial situation is such that the reader can immediately see the difference between what *is* and what most of the characters in the book *think* is. As far as the characters in the book are concerned, what they *think* corresponds to what *is* not so much because they are naive and prone to superstitious explanations, but because the facts themselves seem to give credence to their interpretations. Mikszáth handles this dual "reality" (the reality the reader sees as opposed to the reality the characters choose to live in) with delicate, gentle irony. Hardly does Father János Bélyi, the young impoverished priest, move to Glogova when, unknown to him, his mother dies. When the judge of the village sends the infant Veronika to her brother, Father Bélyi not only learns of his mother's recent death but also of a new, unexpected responsibility which, under his present circumstances, he is hopelessly inept to fulfill adequately. It is at this point that, leaving the sleeping child in front of his door, he goes inside his church and prays to Christ for a "miracle" (II, 24).

While Father Bélyi is inside the church praying, a quick rain storm comes and goes during which an unknown hand places a decrepit, red umbrella over Veronika. And it is when the priest begins to make inquiries concerning the umbrella's proper owner that the fertile imagination of the village folk invents the "legend." One witness claims to have seen the umbrella "descend from heaven" itself (II, 25). The fact that this particular witness is not too reliable (she is known to take a drink now and then) seems to make no difference with respect to her credibility. Her credibility, the narrator mischievously remarks, is founded upon the fact that her husband sprouted a thick beard after his death. This event is somehow said to have bestowed special psychic powers on the old woman. By the time the sexton states that he has seen an old Jew peddler come that way with the red umbrella, and by the time others claim to have seen this particular peddler also, it is too late; reality has no chance against the much more appealing fiction of the umbrella's heavenly origin. In fact, other witnesses soon claim that the old Jew not only bore a significant resemblance to the picture of St. Peter in their church, but that (yes, they remember it well now) there was also something very like a halo around his head (II, 27).

This "legend" is enough to change Veronika's fortune. Her welfare is suddenly the "fashion" of the day. The "women of the village" bake and cook whatever they can afford just to keep the little girl well fed (II, 27). Soon the old widow, whose husband has sprouted a beard after his death, volunteers to be the young priest's cook without pay (and according to the village folk this is in itself a miracle, II, 29). What finally roots the "legend" of the umbrella firmly in the priest's own conscience as well (the priest at first merely tolerates all this "foolishness" with a benign smile) is when an apparently dead man "returns" to life presumably because of the umbrella's miraculous powers (II, 35). After this event the priest himself begins to think that perhaps the umbrella has been sent from heaven in answer to his prayer (II, 36–37). In any event, the umbrella's presence changes everything at Glogova, and by the time this first section of the book ends the village as a whole is ready to take commercial advantage of the religious "miracles." Mikszáth remains neutral with respect to this unholy alliance between the sacred and profane; he seems to accept it as part and parcel of human nature, or, at least, as something to be benignly tolerated.

The second part of the novel is an account of the "true" story of St.

Peter's umbrella. As is customary with Mikszáth, this part takes us further back in time in an attempt to adequately prepare the reader for the total significance of the umbrella's story. In his prime, Pál Gregorics becomes the victim of an insatiable desire for popularity (II, 39). Nothing that he does, however, can gain for him what he so ardently desires: a good reputation. When he smokes expensive cigars, he is said to be "prodigal"; when he changes to a cheap variety, he is said to be "stingy" (II, 40). When (being rich enough not to) he does not work, he is said to be "superfluous"; when he offers his services to the town's government, he is said to be "ready to take the living away from some poor man" (II, 41–42), and so on. His luck with the fairer sex is equally bad. Just as Pál Gregorics is at his wit's end, the 1849 War of Independence breaks out. Since he is too weak to serve in any other capacity, he volunteers to be a spy. And here is where the umbrella comes into the story. According to the narrator, old veterans still remember the "man with the red umbrella" (II, 45). Apparently, in his capacity as spy, Gregorics used the hollowed handle of his umbrella for the conveyance of secret messages and important documents.

Upon his return to Besztercebánya, Gregorics becomes a recluse and a misanthrope. It is at this time that he begets his illegitimate son upon his servant, Anna Wibra, and that his greedy relatives begin to fear that Gregorics's wealth will go to his "bastard" rather than to them. At first Gregorics makes no bones about loving his son, but soon (suspecting foul play on the part of his relatives) he becomes ever more shrewd and calculating. As Gyuri grows up, Gregorics begins to sell large portions of his property in order to turn his wealth into ready cash which he hopes he will be able to hand over to his son prior to his death. He pretends to make business trips to Bohemia and elsewhere when in reality he is visiting his son who is being educated in various parts of the country (including Budapest). The umbrella is always with him, and when Gyuri finds this a constant source of embarrassment, Gregorics lets slip some mysterious hints about how Gyuri " 'will understand one day, when [he] grows up,' " about how the umbrella will come in handy " 'against the rains' " (II, 55, 56). On one occasion, when Gregorics drops the umbrella in a river, he offers an exorbitant reward for its recovery. But this apparently unreasonable attachment to his umbrella merely makes Gregorics more of an eccentric in the eyes of his son as well as in the eyes of the world.

Ironically, Gregorics's shrewd maneuvers and secret plots do not lead to success. They do succeed in totally misleading his greedy relatives, but they do not permit him to hand his wealth over to his son according to his plans. Again, Mikszáth's narrative technique is to pile anecdote-like episode upon anecdote-like episode until it becomes clear to the reader just how lovingly protective and protectively shrewd Gregorics really is. Not being a misanthrope without reason, Gregorics is highly cognizant of the darker side of human nature, particularly of its avaricious side. A few days before his death, and in the utmost secrecy, Gregorics hires two masons to wall up a large, extremely heavy container in the house he intends to pass on to his son. He knows that in spite of a lifelong bribe, the masons' greed will force them to sell this information to Gregorics's relatives, and this is precisely his plan. When the greedy relatives finally acquire the house, the large, heavy container turns out to contain nothing but rusty nails and pieces of junk. Mikszáth, of course, keeps this last bit of information from his readers, so that the readers find out the truth at the same time the greedy relatives do. This has the effect of suddenly putting the late Gregorics in an entirely new perspective. Although already sympathetic to his readers, in retrospect he becomes even smarter and more knowledgeable about human nature than he seemed before.

Gregorics's plan to enrich his illegitimate son notwithstanding his greedy relatives fails merely because of a minor circumstance beyond his control. When Gregorics feels that his end is near, his servant (and the mother of his child) thinks that the old man is speaking nonsense. Consequently, she does not think much of not sending the telegram that would rush Gyuri back to his father's bedside. The little "lie [that the telegram has been sent] consoles" (II, 61) the dying Gregorics enough to enable him to carry the previously described plot to a successful completion, but it cannot keep him in this world beyond his appointed time. Upon his death, the old umbrella (along with a number of other miscellaneous items) is sold at an auction where it is bought by the old Jew peddler who will (after some years) place it over the sleeping Veronika in the remote Slovak village of Glogova.

However, the story of greed is not yet over. At the time of Gregorics's death the contention among the relatives of the deceased is high and vicious. Part of the contention exudes into a litigation somewhat reminiscent of Charles Dickens's great case (Jarndyce vs.

Jarndyce) in *Bleak House*, and it ends in the selfsame way. By the time it is over it no longer matters who wins or loses. Thus, as the Gregorics clan slowly dies out, the "true" inheritance is passed on to "fairy tales. These determine its fate freely; these consume or enlarge it; these place it here or there, according to their own whims" (II, 91).

Meanwhile Gyuri Wibra grows into manhood and, following in his father's footsteps, becomes an eminent lawyer. But his life is never allowed to take its normal course, for his mind is secretly obsessed by the "unfortunate legend of the inheritance" (II, 94). What torments him more than anything else is the unlikelihood of the fortune's simple disappearance from the face of the earth. He travels far and wide and holds numerous investigative conferences with his father's former associates, but all he can learn (and this from his mother) is that at the time of Gregorics's death his father intended to hand the fortune over to him, had he been present. At one point he encounters a dying man who recollects his father's activities during the War of Independence and who talks of the umbrella with the hollow handle as the depository and conveyor of secret documents. In a sudden flash Gyuri realizes the significance of the umbrella, and his father's cryptic words concerning it fall into place. The question now is, is the umbrella still in existence and if so, where? Now that the secret of Gregorics's umbrella is in his possession, Gyuri has no choice but to unravel the tangled threads of its story.

At this point *Szent Péter esernyöje* becomes a veritable detective novel with Gyuri acting as both Sherlock Holmes and Dr. Watson. Pouring over the documents pertaining to the execution of the Gregorics will, he finally stumbles upon this cryptic clue: "*useless objects 2 forints. Purchased by the white Jew*" (II, 99, italics Mikszáth's). Assuming that the old umbrella got lumped with these "useless objects," Gyuri begins his long and frequently frustrated chase, first for the identity of the mysterious "white Jew," then for the whereabouts of the peddler's still living relatives, and, finally, for the last days of the peddler's itinerary among the remote Slovak villages of Northeastern Hungary. It is during these searches that he runs into Veronika, not knowing that his precious umbrella is in her custody, or, rather, in the custody of the parish at Glogova.

The encounter between the future husband and wife is itself fraught with frustrating delays and elating pleasantries, but the pattern of the "fairy tale" that *Szent Péter esernyöje* ultimately is becomes ever more apparent and meaningful. At this point the two basic threads of the story (Gyuri's search for one fortune and his finding another) are interwoven in such a way that they run simultaneously with one another until the thread carrying Gyuri's hopes for riches finally disintegrates. Gyuri makes the connection between his own story and that of Veronika's miraculous umbrella at the famous dinner scene where the "legend" of St. Peter's umbrella is invoked time and again. When one of his dinner partners refers to the "legend" as extremely beautiful and moving, Gyuri's response is: " 'Ah, poor legends . . . if we were to blow the golden gilt, the holy fragrance, the smoke of mystery off one of these legends, what strange, what indifferent truths would be left at the bottom' " (II, 155–56).

Once in possession of the true whereabouts of his umbrella, Gyuri is thrown into a conflict between his newfound desire for Veronika and his age-old obsession with his lost riches. As a lawyer, he is tormented by the multitudinous possibilities of the legality or illegality of his claim (II, 161–62), but as a lover and dreamer the night supplies him with an acceptable way out of his difficulties. He dreams of St. Peter who advises him to marry Veronika and thus obtain the umbrella (II, 164). With this twist in the plot, Gyuri, who up to this point, regarded the St. Peter story as "ridiculous superstition," weaves his own story into it and begins to wish for a "romantic" solution, the kind one finds "in novels," for example (II, 172).

The rest of the novel, although rapidly reaching its inevitable happy ending, is not without further difficulties and further revelations of heretofore undisclosed information. Notwithstanding Mikszáth's dual plot, which constantly allows the reader to distinguish between the fictitious (the St. Peter "legend") and the real (the Gregorics story), the bit of information upon which the plot will finally turn is as carefully guarded from the reader as it is kept from Gyuri himself. The lovers' idyll is itself flooded by the troubled waters of reality when Veronika eavesdrops upon a conversation which causes her to misconstrue Gyuri's true intentions. Even before learning the final truth concerning his umbrella Gyuri reflects upon the fact that he is not "dreaming," that although his potential happiness with Veronika is "more incredible than a novel, still it is reality," that these last occurrences are "miracles [indeed, for] while one legend (that of the umbrella's) was broken, another [that of love's] rose to take its place" (II, 186–87). It is the heretofore undisclosed information that allows Gyuri to vindicate the purity of his intentions with respect to Veronika. When he finds that his umbrella's old wooden handle had been years ago replaced with a new silver one, and when he finds that the old handle had been burnt in a superstitious ceremony to effect one last miraculous cure, his illusions are finally shattered, and, freed from his dreams of greed, he can finally devote his whole being to his dreams of love.

Szent Péter esernyöje combines a unique narrative technique with a significant temporal emphasis, the purpose of which is to separate and reunite the thematic repulsion and attraction between the Romantic fable and the Realistic history. In terms of its temporal unfolding, the story of the umbrella involves three different sequences. The first (of which not much is said in the novel but which is very important nevertheless) is the use to which the umbrella is originally put. Pál Gregorics uses the umbrella to assist in Hungary's War of Independence against Austrian imperialism. This is certainly part of a noble as well as of a Romantic undertaking. Once the war is lost, once Hungary is forced into the Dual Monarchy, Gregorics holds onto the umbrella as a cherished relic of its former glory. As time goes on, however, the umbrella changes its function so that its secret hiding place becomes the hollow in which a fortune is stashed away against the greedy onslaught of avaricious relatives. In its second temporal sequence, therefore, the umbrella becomes the means of an essentially commercial plot. This commercial plot is not in itself dishonorable, but it is certainly tainted by the disreputable avarice that constantly surrounds it and against which it remains an anonymous stronghold. The third temporal sequence of the umbrella's story (though according to the novel's own chronology this is the first) elevates this lowly object to the status of a legend. Although it lacks supernatural powers, the supernatural powers attributed to it become, for all practical purposes, real. The changes it brings about in the life of an orphan, as well as the changes it brings to an entire community, are undeniably beneficial and "miraculous."

Mikszáth's rearrangement of these temporal sequences to fit the thematic structure of his novel is in itself highly revealing. The Romantic fable begins and, in a sense, closes the narrative. Sandwiched between the outer layers of this fabulous frame is the long and detailed account of the commercial vicissitudes surrounding Gregorics's failed plot to save his fortune for his illegitimate son.

In this portion of the book a valuable contrast is provided for the reader by the hints of the once glorious use to which the umbrella had also been put. This fits in well with the thematic drift of the story which, while it constantly tantalizes with the promise of literal riches, is all the while moving toward the bestowing of greater riches, the riches of unselfish love.

According to one of its critics, in the Mikszáthian world only "those find the beauty of life and its true riches who are able to disentangle themselves from the suffocating net of individual interests, who, in the radiance of pure and noble sentiments, are able to shed the coating of selfishness, who [in short] learn to live for others."[6] Another critic speaks of the "eccentricities" and "anecdotes" in which the novel abounds as an "obstacle to [its] realism,"[7] but this is essentially a misunderstanding of the story's overall thematic drift. Clearly, the novel uses its Romantic fable as a means by which to triumph over historical truth paradoxically by protecting a greater historical truth, one that transcends and thereby transforms the barren, everyday world of the Austro-Hungarian Empire. In *Szent Péter esernyöje* the fabulous wins over the realistic by diffusing the latter with its fanciful light and by endowing it with a meaning it would never be able to generate on its own.

III Prakovszky, a siket kovács *(1895–96)*

In the case of *Prakovszky, a siket kovács (Prakovszky, the Deaf Smith)*, a brief outline of the plot can be highly misleading. This short novel, written in twenty serial installments and first published in book form in 1897, is woven from Mikszáth's own childhood memories. In terms of its interior landscape it is an idyllic account of an adolescent's first infatuation with a village beauty. Beyond the first-person narration, however, there emerges the nostalgic world of Protestant Sundays in rural Hungary, the story of an adult love intrigue, and the tragic clash between love and greed that intrudes upon the idyllic atmosphere of this world and destroys it forever.

This short novel is in many ways reminiscent of modernistic perspectivism, that is, of works that rely heavily upon the point of view of a limited narrator, as in the works of Henry James, or that piece a story together by the juxtaposition of a number of different perspectives, as in the stories of Joseph Conrad. It is also a masterpiece of the indirect narration I have briefly discussed earlier. In a sense, the "hero" of the story (Prakovszky, the deaf smith) remains a peripheral character till the very end. The center of the reader's attention is focused on the narrator himself, who in recounting the story of his first love slowly paves the way for the climax of the novel in which Prakovszky, the deaf smith, "hears" the gunshot that ends his son's life in a distant land.

As in *Beszterce ostroma,* in this novel, too, the story ends with the suicide of one of its protagonists, but here the act of self-murder is left behind the scenes, together with the forces that motivate it and bring it about. Through the disintegration of the adolescent idyll that the novel explores, the reader is allowed to glimpse into the merciless world of adulthood in such a way that *Prakovszky* finally emerges as an initiation rite, a myth that pinpoints and also demythologizes the threshold between boyhood and manhood.

Much of the story is punctuated by the Sunday services that begin and end the novel and that connect its various parts as periods connect the sentences that gradually form the unity of a text. These Sunday services, in turn, invoke the families of the principal characters whose destinies are thus both separate from and part of the community of families that form the backdrop of the entire novel. In *Prakovszky* no character stands or has his or her meaning alone; each is part of a family and each family is part of a community, and each community is (presumably) part of larger communities still. The indirect narration here has very much the same effect as the ever widening circles on the surface of a body of water into which a pebble has been cast. The important family members associated with the narrator are his grandfather and his mother; the important role in Piroska Gáll's life is played by her father (and to a lesser extent by her mother); and then there is Prakovszky's son, a lieutenant in the Hungarian Army, a dashing hussar officer, whom the deaf smith loves tenderly and of whom he is inordinately but justifiably proud. The main characters of the story, the characters around whose interwoven destinies the novel revolves, are the narrator, Piroska Gáll (with whom the narrator is infatuated), and Sándor Prakovszky, the hussar officer (with whom Piroska is in love).

The ever widening familial circles out of which the principal characters issue are, in turn, placed into the larger context of the annual cycles. In fact, the story uses the ritual unfolding of a single year (from spring to spring), but the second spring, instead of bringing renewal of life, intrudes upon the ritualistic sequence of nature with the harsh note of Sándor's behind-the-scenes suicide. Thus, the discordant tone of death undermines the myth of human life as in some sense part and parcel of the life of nature.

Mikszáth prepares for the destruction of this nostalgic pagan-like serenity of rural existence by the presence of evil which utilizes the Christian myth of the Fall. The Fall is actually reenacted in an early episode of the story with gentle irony interlarded with parodic elements, but the potential evil it conjures up cannot ever again be completely dispensed with. What leads to the reenactment of the Fall is the narrator's wishful misconstruction of Piroska's amorous glances during the Sunday service that introduces the story. Thinking that the glances are meant for him when in fact they are meant for Sándor who stands behind him, the narrator follows Piroska into a melon field where he sees her deposit a letter. The letter, really a note arranging for the next secret meeting between Piroska and Sándor, is of course not meant for the narrator at all. The narrator, however, does not have time to actually read the note and thus learn the truth, for Sándor shows up and promptly takes possession of it. The reenactment of the Fall occurs when the narrator's grandfather is forced to borrow some money from Piroska's father. During the visit to the Gáll family, Piroska is told to show the narrator the family's garden.

The reenactment of the Fall (which occurs in a chapter entitled "Eve and the Apple") is both obvious and gently humorous, but this does not save it from the element of intentional deception which (however innocent) sounds the first discordant note in the otherwise idyllic atmosphere of the story. Piroska, having seen the narrator take the letter intended for Sándor, does not know that the lieutenant has promptly taken possession of it. She is worried that the narrator may in some way publicize her incipient affair, and she is bent upon stopping this by one means or another. When the narrator's remarks reveal the truth, Piroska allows the narrator to draw a whole series of false inferences. The narrator is, of course, more than happy to accept the fiction of Piroska's love for him, and he is more than willing to abide by the rather strange conditions she puts upon the possibility of further development between them. She is, in fact, tempting the narrator to secrecy with the tantalizing promise of her future graces. When the narrator inquires about future meetings between himself and the girl, Piroska tells him that " 'time takes care of everything. You must be smart and quiet, for if you so much as breathe one word of any of this, of the letter, the lieutenant, or of this very conversation, you will never again speak with me in this life' " (II, 249). It is at this point in the story that Piroska plucks an apricot and, eating half of it herself, offers the other half to the narrator, almost as a sign of their new bond or covenant.

The narrator, writing from the vantage point of more than twenty years (he tells us that at the time of the writing he is "over forty," II, 262), draws an explicit connection between this garden episode of his youth and its original counterpart in Eden: "This is the way Eve must have offered the apple to Adam. But while Eve did it for Adam to know everything, Piroska did it to keep me from knowing anything. Yet paradise was lost here as well as there immediately upon consuming the fruit" (II, 249–50). This last remark is a humorous preface to the following scene which instantaneously transforms the preceding scene from the ridiculous to the sublime. The narrator's paradise, at this point, is lost simply because the young couple is called in for lunch. Little does the narrator know that he has already lost the greater paradise of Piroska's love before ever possessing it. As fanciful and self-consciously parodic as this little reenactment of the Fall is, it is an adequate portent of the evil which will eventually destroy Piroska's own "paradise" and which will jolt the narrator into the sad reality of manhood.

By the time his summer vacation is over, the narrator's uneasy suspicions about Piroska are fully confirmed. The rumors that torment him all summer long merge with the reality of the situation when, just as he is about to return to school, he stumbles upon Piroska and Sándor in the woods where the couple has been secretly meeting all along. The secrecy of these meetings is necessitated by the fact that Piroska's family is well-to-do as well as by the fact that old Prakovszky dislikes Piroska's father. The smith's dislike is well founded, for Master Gáll is petulant, selfish, and incredibly greedy. Although we get several glimpses into the potentially destructive force behind this selfishness and greed, the reader's attention is still on the narrator and on the narrator's certain movement toward maturity. This movement toward maturity is punctuated by his disengagement from the tormenting infatuation with Piroska.

Looking back at the "story of [his] first love," the narrator places it in the context of natural cycles: "everyone felt the warm breezes of spring. Perhaps others were luckier than I, for I received but one ray of sunlight while they may have received many, whole spectrums of them, but the result is the same. The first sunshine of spring is beautiful precisely because it is not yet real, because it is but a mere flash, a promise, an early messenger that breathes on frostbitten fields, that thaws out frozen hearts, and then, like a dream, disintegrates" (II, 271). A similar sentiment is expressed at the end of the chapter in which the narrator finds Piroska and Sándor in their secret meeting place: the narrator looks back at the diminishing woods and exclaims, "How large the world is! And in this large world how many more beautiful girls than my Piroska!" (II, 280).

This idyllic maturity, however, is not the real maturity the narrator will be granted by the tragic ending of his story. With the next spring arrives the beginning of a new summer vacation. But this new vacation will not be the time for a new idyll. The discordant note of greed will undermine it completely, and Sándor's reported suicide will make the world seem a very unfit place for any idylls—past, present, or future. Master Gáll's greed will not only disregard his daughter's happiness, it will seem unpleasant to the point of incredulity. This description seems to suggest that with the narrator's return from school his style changes from Romantic lightness to Realistic heaviness, but this is not the case. Mikszáth retains the indirection of his narration to the very end.

The story remains light and indirect even in its treatment of Master Gáll's greed. The reader comes to see this greed bit by bit and in such a way that it seems to remain the butt of gentle satire. The narrator's grandfather becomes furious when Master Gáll demands repayment of the loan mentioned earlier. When the narrator accompanies his grandfather to the Gáll estate, the reader learns that Piroska's father "needs" the money for the world is "perverse enough" to have the bride's family pay for the wedding. We also see that Gáll is not too concerned with his daughter's happiness (present or future) for, as he puts it, " 'what do I get out of her happiness?' " (II, 287). Even the fact that Gáll picks the bridegroom because the latter had purchased land from him which turned out to have valuable coal deposits and which, by hook or by crook, Gáll intends to bring back into the family, does not succeed in changing the light, satiric mood of the narration. Gáll's acute frustrations remain, ultimately, entertainingly humorous. The picture of his greed is so exaggerated as to be a caricature, and this tends to distract the reader from Gáll's otherwise appalling avarice. By this mode of narration Mikszáth can deliver his "punchline" with a force that shocks, and this is certainly to his credit. What is not to Mikszáth's credit (and, indeed, this is the one serious flaw in *Prakovszky*) is that Sándor's suicide is ultimately not believable, not unless the reader is ready to believe that a dashing hussar officer will end his life simply because a girl turns him down.

Despite this serious flaw, however, the ending of *Prakovszky* is a powerful one. During the Sunday service, in the course of which Piroska's banns are first announced, Prakovszky, the deaf smith, "hears" a gunshot. Although the old man is frantic and keeps rushing about in search of another ear that has also heard it, this episode is the last joke in the novel. The entire community is in an uproar at the idea that the *deaf* smith claims to have *heard* something no one else heard, until the news comes that on that particular Sunday Sándor Prakovszky had shot himself in the head. The last words of the story are spoken by the narrator's mother who tells her son that a " 'parent's heart can see farther than eye can see, and hear better than ear can hear. You do not know this yet' " (II, 300).

Thus Mikszáth has once again contrasted materialistic values with nonmaterialistic ones; but unlike in his previous novels, in *Prakovszky* he achieves his effect by springing the unexpected ending upon his readers out of, as it were, nowhere. As I have indicated at the outset of this discussion, however, this is not quite the case. The contrast between the pagan-like serenity of rural existence and the quasiparodic reenactment of the Fall is enough to prepare the reader for *accepting* the tragic end, even while it is not enough for allowing the reader to *anticipate* it. Furthermore, the sudden reversal in mood achieved by the ending of *Prakovszky* is in keeping with its theme. The step from boyhood to manhood does not come with chronological age, but with the unexpected shock of recognition that the world is not a playground after all, but a battlefield on which the innocent do not always win and the guilty do not always lose.

IV Két választás Magyarországon *(1896–97)*

Két választás Magyarországon (Two Elections in Hungary) holds a unique place in Mikszáth's canon in that it consists of several independent narratives (two short novels and a short story) subsequently put together to form the present novel (1910). The whole story is prefigured by a series of satiric letters first published in the *Pesti*

Hirlap (Budapest Gazette) in 1893–94. The letters are written by a fictitious member of parliament, Menyhért Katánghy, and, although they are addressed to his wife (Klára), the editors of the paper consider them newsworthy because of their politically informative value. The fictitious Menyhért Katánghy is a *mameluk*, a representative sycophantically supportive of the existing government. The *mameluk* of the latter half of the nineteenth century is so called because of his staunch alliance with the "establishment" as against the Party of the Opposition. "The Letters of the Right Honorable Menyhért Katánghy, Member of the House of Representatives" form a necessary prelude to *Két választás Magyarországon* in that the novel's provenance is indebted to them. The novel's *raison d'être*, its entire narrative framework, is the immediate result of the notoriety of these letters. Since the narrator of the novel is presumably Kálmán Mikszáth himself (although, again, it is clear that this is a pose, an ingeniously clever fictional ploy), *Két választás Magyarországon* is both about the political scene of the latter half of the nineteenth century and about its own provenance, about its own writing of itself.

"The Letters of the Right Honorable Menyhért Katánghy" expose their author both as politician and as private individual. As a politician, Menyhért Katánghy is shown to be a sycophantic opportunist, while as a private individual he is shown to be a deceitful man and husband. As a politician, his characteristic pose is struck in the first letter where he informs his wife (and the readership of the paper for which he writes) that the "government is healthy . . . all the signs augur well; only their interpreters differ and [tend to be] malicious" (XIV, 481). As a private individual and husband, his characteristic trait is revealed in the first as well as in subsequent postscripts where he constantly reminds his wife of his frequent but inevitably frustrated attempts to find a suitable place to rent. He blames his inability to find a dwelling on an implied apartment shortage. Thus, indirectly, his readers learn that he intends to have a good time in the capital by keeping his wife in the country. Menyhért Katánghy shows himself to be a pleasure-seeker in the guise of a concerned and anxious family man. His politics are equally ambivalent, and their ambivalence is best manifested by the twelfth letter, one of Mikszáth's minor masterpieces of satire.

Before the satiric qualities of this letter can be appreciated, a few words will have to be said about its historical context. At the time of

Kossuth's death there is a movement in Hungary to bring the great patriot's body home and bury it with full honors. Kossuth, having been the key figure in the War of Independence against Austria, is *persona non grata* (even in death) from the point of view of Francis Joseph I, Emperor of Austria and King of Hungary.

In this last letter to his wife, Katánghy attempts to justify his voting against Kossuth's burial with full honors. His justification is a political tour de force in which Katánghy explains that his vote *against* Kossuth is really a revolutionary vote *for* the integrity of the great patriot's memory. To force the King to acquiesce to a burial with full honors (which in itself would be an impossibility, as Katánghy explains) would elevate the King's reputation at the expense of the former Hungarian leader's. As "Kossuth had never anticipated such a benefice from the King, as he had always wanted his greatness without it," by voting against him the *mameluk* claims to have voted for him (XIV, 545). It is to Mikszáth's credit as a satirist that in exposing Katánghy's convoluted logic he almost makes it credible in spite of its obviously contorted argument. Katánghy's ambivalence is thus at once deplorable and understandable. It is deplorable in that it reveals a base lack of conviction, and it is understandable in that it shows that qua politician, Katánghy is a universally recognizable opportunist and hypocrite.

The first of the originally independent narratives that comprise *Két választás Magyarországon* purports to be Katánghy's biography. It chronicles his entry into politics following his unsuccessful attempt at earning his fortune as a medical doctor. The story of the second election is the chronicle of Katánghy's machinations to gain a second district for his political career after his failure to hold on to the first. Both stories expose the vicissitudes of a complicated political machinery which is able to sustain the fiction of democracy, the illusion that its elected members are actually chosen by the public at large. Although *Két választás Magyarországon* abounds in specific allusions to actual contemporary figures and although (in spite of its necessarily exaggerated qualities) it is a relatively accurate account of the political life of post-Compromise Hungary, its insightful treatment of general political chicanery, its tongue-in-cheek implication that politics is mostly a type of confidence game, renders it of considerable universal significance.

The first chapter of the novel proper (which is entitled "A Chapter That Does Not Belong to This History") immediately sets the pace for the kind of self-referring bravado in which *Két választás Magyarországon* abounds. The ploy Mikszáth utilizes here is reminiscent of certain novelistic practices of the eighteenth century (such as those of Daniel Defoe or Henry Fielding) which deny their own fictionality, insisting that their authors are either editors or compilers of authentic memoirs or documents. But Mikszáth expands upon this ploy by placing a fictitious version of himself inside his story as well as by relying upon the kind of perspectivism we find later in such works as Conrad's *Lord Jim*. The novel opens with a reference to the Katánghy letters of a few years ago and to the author's animosity toward Katánghy both because of the latter's former success as a writer and because of his attempt to keep his wife at bay by claiming inability to find a suitable dwelling in the capital.

The immediate reasons for "Mikszáth's" taking up his pen, however, are both more complicated and more amusing than this. First, the author remarks upon the fact that Katánghy, although "relatively famous by now, has never been seen inside the editorial offices" of the *Pesti Hirlap*. This gives rise to the speculation that perhaps "this Katánghy doesn't even exist" (II, 306). Soon the letters that pour into the editor's office raise certain questions and form certain hypotheses. One of these hypotheses reads: "Is it not possible that our own talented Kálmán Mikszáth writes under the Katánghy name?" (II, 307). It is this hypothesis that angers the author (whose initials are, by the way, the same as those of Menyhért Katánghy's except in reverse order) and causes him to exclaim that he shall "no longer let this renegade hide behind the milestone between existence and nonexistence," and that he shall be forced to "rip the veil off his [Katánghy's] past and present" (II, 307–08). Thus, "Mikszáth's" immediate motive for writing is self-vindication. He wishes to disclaim authorship of the Katánghy letters that appeared in the *Pesti Hirlap* a few years prior to the writing of the present work, and he wishes to show that Menyhért Katánghy does exist, that he is a "real flesh-and-blood person." He is also aware of the fact that he is specifically addressing himself to an audience capable of "discrediting what is real and of accepting what is impossible" (II, 309).

Furthermore, as one of the paper's subscribers has demanded that Katánghy's full biography be published in the *Pesti Hirlap*, and as "Mikszáth" himself is associated with this particular paper, the editors commission him to satisfy the demands of the readership and produce the requested biography. Now the author's problem is one of adequate sources for his undertaking. Fortunately, however, he makes the acquaintance of an aunt of Katánghy's wife and of Katánghy's manservant, both of whom supply the author with more than adequate information. The concluding words of the first chapter are indicative of the extent to which the self-referring bravado of which the "novel" consists is willing to go: "And now, having given a conscientious account of my sources, with the help of the gods and muses that be I shall commence my biography—may [my dear readers] be kind enough to blindly credit my words" (II, 311).

Having established this self-referring framework, Mikszáth now turns to the "Story of the First Election" in which he gives a full account of Katánghy's early life, courtship, and marriage, and of his entry into the political life of post-Compromise Hungary. Katánghy, being of gentry origin, is forced to earn a living. In order to find a situation that involves little work and a potentially lucrative existence, he decides to become a fashionable doctor at a well-respected Austrian resort. His entry into this highly competitive and risky field bears all the characteristics of a well-designed confidence game. In an attempt to establish himself as a sought-after healer, Katánghy resorts to the fiction of a substantial clientele. He makes certain that the entire community sees him rushing about, going from nonexistent patient to nonexistent patient at all hours of the day and night. Unfortunately his game is so successful that it becomes a virtual failure. He makes quite an impression at the resort, but his potential *real* clients shy away from approaching him for his services precisely because the new doctor seems too busy to take on new patients. There is, however, one potential patient who insists on obtaining Katánghy's attention. This is Klára, the doctor's future wife.

With this new turn in the plot, the novel takes on a new dimension. The story of Katánghy's courtship and of his subsequent marriage is the satiric repetition of the Moll Flanders syndrome. Both Katánghy and his future wife are in search of a wealthy marriage partner, and each thinks that the other represents what he or she seeks. The innumerable traps, innuendoes, and resultant misinterpretations weave the destinies of these characters in and out of the inevitable pattern of a mutually exclusive confidence game. Because of the enticing hints dropped by Klára's mother and because of the substantial fee Katánghy receives, the bridegroom-to-be has every reason to believe that his present client would bring substantial riches along with the obvious riches of her beauty into their marriage. Not thinking of the possibility that Klára's motives may be identical with his own, being too preoccupied with his own potential "good" fortune, Katánghy becomes the victim of his own design. It is only after the wedding that both husband and wife realize the truth. To Katánghy's credit, however, he accepts his fate graciously. Immediately following upon the long discussion in which each learns the truth about the other, Katánghy simply says: " 'Well, wife, we have found one another. We deserve it. But now let's go to lunch' " (II, 362).[8]

Katánghy's entry into political life is also owing to a well-designed confidence game, but with this difference: here the plans for the doctor's future meet with unprecedented success. One of Klára's relations, a mayor in a remote Transylvanian town, goes about to prepare the political future of his new in-law with all the exhilarating joy of an incorrigible gambler. The mayor, being unpopular in his district, pretends to be *against* Katánghy, and it is precisely this ploy that compels the doctor's future constituency to cast its unanimous vote *for* him.

Mikszáth's narrative in this section of the book is characterized by ironic detachment. The political chicanery he explores emerges almost as if it were meant to emerge in spite of rather than because of Mikszáth's pen. This lends an atmosphere of objectivity to the narrator's researches into Katánghy's past as well as into the workings of political life in post-Compromise Hungary. The illusion that a politician works for the benefit of the public is undermined by the actuality of political manipulation which succeeds in misleading the public into giving its wholehearted support to the politician's self-interest. As the Katánghy letters have already indicated, a politician (once he is securely established) reaps the financial benefits of his office without having to exert himself. His sole responsibility seems to be to maintain the illusion of public benefit his office is said to guarantee.

The first major section of the novel, the story of Katánghy's first election, maintains the fiction of reportage. Another way of putting this would be to say that this section of the novel is supposed to be read as though it were a series of newspaper articles. This is in keeping with the initial fiction whereby "Mikszáth" takes upon himself the task of writing a biography of Katánghy for the sake of disclaiming authorship of the Katánghy letters and for the sake of proving the politician's existence. With this ploy Mikszáth manages to expose the political scene of post-Compromise Hungary in such a way that all further exposure seems to become superfluous. Once a characteristic instance is given, why bother with further applications of the same basic principle?

At this point the self-referential scheme of the novel's provenance reestablishes the illusion of the story's reality. Having interested the readership of the *Pesti Hirlap* by giving an account of Katánghy's entry into political life, the fortunes and misfortunes of Katánghy's further career continue to remain in the center of the public's curiosity. Just as the publication of the story of Katánghy's first election comes to a successful conclusion, it comes to the author's attention that the new representative of the remote Transylvanian district has just lost his office and that he has already gained a new one, in an entirely different part of the country.

This new development succeeds in casting an aura of mystery around Katánghy's figure in such a way that it renews the reader's interest in the remainder of his story. Why has Katánghy lost his ingeniously gained office, and how has he managed to find a new one in such a short period of time? When the editors of the *Pesti Hirlap* reappoint "Mikszáth" for the writing of the story of this second election, the author finds himself unable to come up with a satisfactory explanation for this new twist in his "hero's" career. At this point he consults Katánghy himself, but the politician refuses to divulge any information for fear that a further exposé may totally discredit him. When the editors insist that he fulfill his obligation to the paper by writing the story of the second election, "Mikszáth" keeps complaining that he cannot write out of sheer "fantasy," that he is "not God who can create something out of nothing" (II, 412 & 413). When the editor agrees to send special correspondents to the respective parts of the country to dig up the necessary information for "Mikszáth" to continue his articles, the author consents to the writing of the second half of the story.

Since the correspondents require more time than anticipated, however, the story of the second election cannot appear in the pages of the *Pesti Hirlap*. At this point Mikszáth turns his supposed reportage into a "novel" by claiming that "whoever will be still interested in the life story of this splendid statesman, will probably be pleased to read [the story of the second election] in this book, which is not a literary composition but simple reportage, based on information supplied by the three correspondents" (II, 414).

The story of the second election is more complicated than the first and adds a new element to the novel's exposure of the vicissitudes of profound political corruption, particularly of the *mameluk* variety. We learn not just how easily a politician can be made, but also how easily a politician can be unmade as well. In this particular instance Mikszáth accomplishes his design by showing how Katánghy is unmade and how he is remade at the expense of the unmaking of another politician. The situation as it unfolds is briefly as follows: Katánghy loses his office in the remote district of Transylvania because of his wife's interference. Klára is unhappy that her husband "cannot" find a suitable dwelling in the capital and that this necessitates prolonged separation between husband and wife, so she begs the politician's constituency to strip Katánghy of his office. It is, then, the gallantry of the members of his district that is responsible for Katánghy's loss of office.

At this point Mikszáth introduces a subplot which is also a paradigm for Katánghy to follow. In a town in another district of Hungary, the mayor's daughter is engaged to a rising young politician. When a rich suitor comes on the scene, the mayor plots the disengagement of his daughter and carries his plot to a successful completion. This story reaches Katánghy as an interesting anecdote, and its underlying structure becomes the model of his reestablishing himself in the world of politics. If it is possible to oust one bridegroom in order to replace him with another, why cannot this be accomplished with a politician as well? Once this possibility is borne in upon Katánghy, it becomes a veritable obsession. Katánghy begs a minister to assist him in his design. The minister communicates his desire to the mayor of the town in question that Katánghy replace the town's current candidate for political office (who, it should be remembered, is identical with the ousted bridegroom). The mayor discredits the current candidate, pretends to run for office himself, then revokes his candidacy on the basis that the loss of his mayoralty would be a disservice to the town, and, at the last moment, recommends Katánghy for the position of the town's new representative. Needless to say, this confidence game succeeds admirably.

With this "report" concluded, "Mikszáth" feels that he has given an adequate account of Katánghy's career. But the readership of the

Pesti Hirlap is not satisfied. Since it is known that Katánghy has also received an appointment to the treasury, the public demands to know this last stage in the hero's upward move in the world of politics. By, once again, bringing attention to itself as a "report" of recent events, the novel realigns itself with the previously established fiction and can reach its conclusion by the publication of a private letter written by Katánghy to his wife.

"Mikszáth" is haunted by a certain amount of guilt in thus making public the contents of a private letter, but he justifies himself on two counts. This act of justification is somewhat reminiscent of Katánghy's attempt to vindicate himself for having voted against Kossuth's burial with full honors. "Mikszáth" explains that as the letter in question has been lifted from Katánghy's pocket by a fellow correspondent of the *Pesti Hirlap* prior to its being mailed, it cannot be said to constitute a letter at all; rather, it can be looked upon as a series of notes which detail the circumstances of Katánghy's appointment to the treasury. The second justification is a simple appeal to human nature. Once a newspaperman possesses a certain piece of information, "Mikszáth" tells us, it would be unreasonable to expect him to withhold it from his public.

Katánghy's last letter reveals that the political confidence game of post-Compromise Hungary is incorrigible. The situation is briefly as follows: a minister of the government wants Katánghy in a newly vacated office in the treasury because the office is too popular, too much in demand. As the minister rationalizes the situation, were Katánghy to fill this office, it would immediately lose its popularity. When Katánghy's vanity is wounded by this offer, the minister employs the kind of convoluted logic both Katánghy and "Mikszáth" have resorted to in the past. As the minister explains, what appears to be a slur upon Katánghy's integrity is really a compliment in disguise. " 'Where it is necessary to rob an office of its significance, there your ability to accomplish this feat is precisely that power which a true politician must possess' " (II, 488–89). With this argument the minister disarms Katánghy in the same way in which Katánghy (and, on occasion, "Mikszáth" himself) disarms those who try to see through the machinations of political chicanery.

Having brought Katánghy's career up to date, the novel completes its underlying design. The novelistic exposure of political confidence games is combined with the novel's self-exposure in such a way that the thematic drift of the novel assumes a dual function, one side of which illumines the other. The underlying structure in the stories that detail the two elections, as well as in the brief account of Katánghy's appointment to the treasury, reveals a conscious manipulation of appearances for the sake of the manipulator's profit. Each political maneuver involves the fabrication of an appearance the public is deliberately expected to mistake for a reality. Since no political move in *Két választás Magyarországon* is straightforward and open, what the novel implies is that all political moves are games politicians play with appearances they intend to be mistaken for realities.

Paradoxically, Mikszáth's own strategy in the novel is the same as that of his "heroes." In other words, the structure of the act of narration is identical with the structure of the act narrated. There is, however, a significant difference between the act of narration and the act narrated. While in the act narrated the public is expected to mistake an appearance for a reality, in the act of narration the readership of the novel is expected to see *how* an appearance can be so manipulated as to be mistaken for a reality. The manipulators within the novel reap the benefits of their consciously emplotted deceptions. Mikszáth as manipulator of the story reaps a benefit, too, but this benefit is moral rather than monetary.

Like the various "fictions" invented by the politicians within the novel, Mikszáth's fiction is also a lie, but with this significant difference: while the lies of the politicians are designed to remain opaque, Mikszáth's own "lie" is transparent from the beginning. The self-referring, metafictional mode of the act of narration is precisely what disabuses the illusion-making inherent in the nonself-referring, nonmetafictional mode operative throughout in the act narrated. The theme of the novel cannot be disengaged from the thematic drift of its gradual unfolding. It is precisely by remaining self-referring throughout that *Két választás Magyarországon* can become referential as well. It is precisely by constantly bringing attention to itself as fiction that the novel can validate its claim to be making acceptable pronouncements about reality.

V Új Zrinyiász *(1898)*

As Henry Fielding's *Joseph Andrews* is a "comic epic-poem in prose," Mikszáth's *Új Zrinyiász (New Zrinyiad)* is a satiric epic-poem in the guise of a novel. The subtitle of the first edition of the book, "A Satiric Picture of Society and Politics," does not allude to the novel's mock-heroic qualities because the educated Hungarian reader has already been alerted to this aspect of the book by its title. As in *Beszterce ostroma,* Mikszáth's self-proclaimed aim in this novel, too, is to present a "confrontation between medieval practices and current, modern ideologies" (II, 495); but, unlike in *Beszterce ostroma,* here the comparison is not between an archaic hero and his contemporary counterparts, but between a Renaissance knight (duly resurrected for the occasion) and the late nineteenth-century guardians of his heritage.

The protagonist of *Új Zrinyiász* is Count Miklós Zrinyi (1508–66), the heroic but unsuccessful defender of Szigetvár against the Turk. The title of Mikszáth's novel derives its significance from the heroic poem, *Szigeti veszedelem (The Peril of Sziget;* 1651*),* written by the protagonist's great-grandson, Count Miklós Zrinyi, the poet (1620–64). *Szigeti veszedelem,* "also known as the *Zrinyiász,*"[9] is to *Új Zrinyiász* what Homer's *Ulysses* is to *Joseph Andrews.* But while in Fielding's novel the underlying structural analogues to the Homeric epic are easily detectible, in Mikszáth's novel the connection between the new and the old is more tenuous. Like Ulysses, Joseph Andrews is on a journey the desired goal of which is wife and home; but unlike the historic Zrinyi, Mikszáth's fictitiously resurrected version of the national hero can only repeat his former destiny when the novel's *raison d'être* drowns in its own complications.

Miklós Zrinyi's *Szigeti veszedelem* places the heroic struggles of the poet's great-grandfather in a transcendant context. The Turkish menace that engulfs Renaissance Hungary is envisioned in terms of divine punishment. The epic takes its departure from this notion, then rounds off the tragic destiny of its protagonist by returning to it. Within the world of the poem, the "heathen" threat to Hungary is a sign of divine displeasure. Hungary is no longer loyal to the Christian ideals which once made her great, yet the defenders of Sziget (particularly their leader, Count Miklós Zrinyi) are not really representative of this disloyalty. Zrinyi's prayer to God is answered in such a way that the final defeat of the Hungarians at the hands of an overwhelming enemy is really seen as a kind of victory. Zrinyi's historic sortie with two hundred loyal soldiers becomes a symbolic martyrdom, and this martyrdom plants the seed of ultimate "heathen" defeat in spite of its temporary triumph.[10]

The historico-literary background of *Új Zrinyiász,* then, forms a necessary prelude to Mikszáth's plot. The immediate germ of the novel, however, is attributable to a statement made by Wilhelm II, Emperor of Germany, who in the fall of 1897, during a visit to Budapest, compared the nobility of post-Compromise Hungary with Miklós Zrinyi and the heroic heritage of the great Renaissance knight.[11] Mikszáth, increasingly disturbed by the social and political self-delusion around him, responded with *Új Zrinyiász* in an attempt to show the appalling discrepancy between the heroic ideals of the past and their illusory continuance in the present. Notwithstanding the potentially tragic overtones in Mikszáth's overall design, *Új Zrinyiász* remains almost exclusively satiric. Although the satire is biting throughout, the fictitious continuation of Zrinyi's life story continuously avoids the potentially tragic in its thematic unfolding. Even the scenes that involve bloodshed bypass the tragic vicissitudes of violence and maintain their satiric focus on late nineteenth-century bureaucracy. But perhaps this weakness in the novel is necessitated by the very discrepancy between the ancient and the modern *Új Zrinyiász* is trying to explore.

The novel, which consists of two parts, tells the story of Count Miklós Zrinyi and his men after their miraculous resurrection in post-Compromise Hungary. At first the "resurrection" is not credited by the public, but soon the fidelity of the miracle receives the sanction of the authorities, including the authorities of the Catholic Church. Zrinyi and his men become the welcome guests of the new age.

The first part of the novel is the chronicle of Zrinyi's reception by the joyous public and the history of his new career as a banker. Although minor conflicts between the old and the new abound in this section of the novel, there are no serious developments until close to the end of the first part, when one of Zrinyi's men is "forced" by latter-day formalities to fight a duel which ends in the death of his opponent. This tragic note proves to be of some significance with respect to the remainder of the plot.

In the second half of the novel Zrinyi, particularly in his capacity as a banker, continues to run into ever more serious conflicts with aspects of the modern age. He imprisons several of his compatriots and is eventually responsible for the deaths of a number of shareholders. The conflicts that develop as a result of Zrinyi's intention to play the role of a feudal lord against the bureaucratic procedures that run the modern world are eventually solved by a royal dispensation. The novel ends with Zrinyi's return to a fortress, very much like the fortress of Sziget, where, once again, he sacrifices himself for the benefit of his country. Mikszáth, in other words, solves the insoluble conflicts that develop between the forces of the old and the new by resorting to an imaginary attack upon Hungary during which Zrinyi's history can repeat and thus fulfill itself. Although this "clever" solution may at first appear as a flaw in the novel, it is actually the logical conclusion to the conflicts that rise and grow as the plot of the novel develops.

The narrative technique employed in *Új Zrinyiász* is somewhat reminiscent of the narrative behavior we have seen in *Két választás Magyarországon*. This novel also relies heavily on the fiction of reportage, and although here Mikszáth does not place a fictitious version of himself inside the story, the narrator frequently claims to be working with public sources, such as newspaper articles. As one of Mikszáth's critics puts it, *Új Zrinyiász* appears to be the collaboration of the "parliamentary correspondent, the newspaperman, and the artist."[12] And indeed, once the plot receives its impetus from the fiction of the resurrection, the narrator continuously keeps himself in the view of the reader. He quotes newspaper articles, cites public documents (such as parliamentary testimonies), and private letters.

The fiction of the resurrection that begins the novel is itself a delightful narrative ploy. Here the narrator is clearly more than a mere correspondent; here he plays the Romantic role of creator. He sets the plot in motion by "reporting" God's mistake in which the divine author of the universe sends Gabriel to blow his horn to summon the living and the dead for the day of judgment. No sooner does Gabriel begin to blow his horn, however, than an "invisible hand" touches his shoulder (II, 497). Although the summons can be revoked, the initial bursts of the trumpet cannot. Zrinyi and his men rise from their graves. At first those resurrected have no recollection of their previous deaths; slowly, however, they realize that they are either the victims of some "enchantment" or of some "unfathomable divine intent" (II, 503). Shortly after their resurrection, the men from the Renaissance experience their first encounter with modernity when a train rushes by them.

At this point the narrator resorts to the fiction of the gradual acceptance of the "news" of the resurrection. The local papers send numerous telegrams to Budapest, but at first only one paper in the capital responds. And that response is an article about the "Crazed Rural Letterwriters" who insist that Zrinyi and his men have returned from the dead. What bothers the writer of the article in question is the receipt of another telegram which claims that in the cemetery at Sziget a large number of open and empty graves have been discovered. From this the writer of the article deduces that there may be a "causal connection" between the reports of Zrinyi's resurrection and the open graves, and that perhaps "some priestly superstition is in the making [of which] the *Hungarian Government* may be cognizant" (II, 506, italics Mikszáth's). A later article in another paper takes up this issue of "some priestly superstition," and argues that either "the priests and holy writ have been lying to us these nineteen hundred years . . . or we must accept the resurrection of Zrinyi and his men" (II, 510). The Church is, of course, elated with this unexpected proof of its teachings, and by the time a special papal encyclical is written on the subject, the entire population is ready to accept the truth of Zrinyi's resurrection. Throughout all this clamoring for the acceptability of the miracle, the representatives of the Church are not the sole targets of Mikszáth's satire. The "Historical Society" along with numerous bureaucracies all take their fair share in the proceedings.

The end result of all these proceedings is the official and public recognition and acceptance of Zrinyi's miraculous rise from the dead. The plot of the novel can now begin to show, step by step and anecdote by anecdote, the various manifestations of its basic thesis, namely, the hopeless incompatibility "between medieval practices and current, modern ideologies." Although for the most part Mikszáth does not take sides here with the old as opposed to the new, there are important confrontations between the sixteenth and the nineteenth centuries which tend to be critical of the latter. At one point, for example, when Zrinyi is introduced to Artur Görgei (the hero of Hungary's War of Independence against Austria who, in order to save the lives of his men, surrendered his arms at Világos), the Renaissance knight reflects wryly that " 'either I or he, but one of us cannot possibly be a hero' " (II, 537). Later in the plot Zrinyi formulates the incompatibility between his age and that of Mikszáth's contemporaries admirably when, in response to the modern concept of "individual rights," he states: " 'Do what you will with such a state of affairs. In my time you had to respect but one person, the king, and that was uncomfortable enough. But to be mindful [of the rights] of sixteen million persons, why that's intolerable. That's hell itself' " (II, 616–17).

Despite the fact that this novel is not really an attempt to compare the old with the new with the explicit intent of disparaging the latter, *Új Zrinyiász* is nevertheless a bitterly satiric attack on the commercial, social, and bureaucratic powers of post-Compromise Hungary. Although it lacks no amusing anecdotes, the novel seems to suffer somewhat from "thesis-riding," that is, from episodes which seem to have been chosen for the sake of illustrating the points implicit in them. Thus, the remainder of the novel involves a threefold plot along with the arbitrary resolution of an apparently insoluble conflict. The first element of the plot embodies the government's desire to satisfy public opinion by installing Zrinyi in a position appropriate to his rank and historic prestige. Zrinyi is made the director of a new bank the purpose of which, among other things, is to insure landowners against leaving behind mortgaged real estate were they to die prematurely. This "aristocratic" function seems, in the eyes of the public, to render the position worthy of Zrinyi.

The second aspect of the threefold plot involves a title-hungry *nouveau riche* family, the head of which, in order to sell a piece of property for the benefit of Zrinyi's bank, insists on a contractual promise that the great Renaissance hero dine with them every Sunday. It is this insistence on formalities and the illusions they create that are Mikszáth's authentic targets in *Új Zrinyiász*. The means whereby Mikszáth manages to hit this target time and again is the ploy of comparing the old and the new. This way the form can be explicitly compared with the content it no longer has.

A good case in point for this thematic development is the duel between one of Zrinyi's men and his modern counterpart. It appears that shortly after their resurrection a derogatory article is published concerning this member of Zrinyi's retinue. The fact that the content of the article may be true is of no importance whatsoever. What is important is that Zrinyi's man has failed to challenge the author of this article. Because of this failure, he is no longer considered a "gentleman," that is to say, no longer considered to have the right of redressing an insult by means of a formal duel. When he is insulted a second time, this time to his face and consequently to his knowledge, the formalities appertaining to his situation do not permit him to go through with the duel otherwise demanded by the circumstances. It is in this connection that the narrator remarks bitterly: "forms reign here. Forms and nothing but forms. Essences go for nothing, but forms are sacrosanct" (II, 577).

The third element in the threefold plot leads directly to the major conflict and the most bitterly satiric elements in the novel. Zrinyi's innocent (or perhaps not so innocent) flirtations with a married lady, one of the regulars at the Sunday dinners, develops into a full-fledged love affair. The meeting between the hero and the lady in question actually precedes the first Sunday dinner and is somewhat reminiscent of the meeting between the idyllic lovers in *Szent Péter esernyöje*. The lady in question drops a piece of jewelry in a public park; Zrinyi steps on it, breaks it, and is thus forced to replace it out of gallantry. The replacement is, of course, much more valuable than the original. When the lady's impoverished husband attempts to hock the jewel in question, he learns its true value and concludes that his wife has been "unfaithful" to him. Mikszáth seems to have lifted this part of his plot from Guy de Maupassant's short story, "The Jewels." In Mikszáth's novel, however, the theme is not one of ironic reversal whereby what was "false" before is now "true" (the jewels), and what was "true" before is now "false" (the wife); rather, for Mikszáth this aspect of the plot is merely the foundation for the explicit conflict between the feudal hero and his "democratic" brave new world.

When the husband confronts Zrinyi, the Renaissance hero simply imprisons him in the bank's basement. A reporter eventually tracks down the missing husband only to be incarcerated with him. When the whole shameful procedure reaches the ears of the authorities, the major conflict in the novel is prepared for. This is the conflict between the authorities' sycophantic willingness to make allowances for the national hero and their apparent loyalty to the modern concept of individual rights.

Mikszáth takes the plot of his novel here to the point where the reader can no longer be in doubt as to the extent to which bureaucracies will go to have it both ways. Only the ultimate crime, that is, the taking of human life, can jolt the machinations of the authorities into the open. And Zrinyi does commit the ultimate crime. When the shareholders of the bank accuse him of mismanagement, the Renaissance knight calls upon his faithful soldiers to defend his "honor." The fiasco that results entails bloodshed. Many are wounded, and at least one shareholder is murdered. Now the authorities can no longer smooth things over behind the scenes. But what happens before the scenes is not much different from what has been happening behind them to this point. The difference is that now the government has to put on a public show.

Zrinyi is arrested, and an entire parliamentary session is devoted to the political arguments concerning the rights and wrongs of the case. There is a faction that insists on Zrinyi's innocence on the basis that the national hero is a living anachronism who cannot be bound by the laws of the nineteenth century. The public is also on Zrinyi's side. What the parliamentary sessions reveal, however, is the ultimate and irreconcilable incompatibility between individual initiative (such as Zrinyi's) and individual rights (such as Zrinyi's prisoner's).

The plot finds its final resolution in a royal pardon which merely ends the parliamentary debates. As the conflicting sides over which the debate has raged rest on radically opposing fundamentals, they can never be resolved except by some twisting and turning of the formalities to squeeze from them some sort of legal self-satisfaction. But this is not necessary. By royal edict, Zrinyi is allowed to take on a role similar to his role in sixteenth-century Hungary, and Mikszáth can thus allow him to repeat his historic mission by once again permitting him to sacrifice himself for his country. The fictitious war that ends the novel undoes, as it were, the divine error responsible for Zrinyi's resurrection in the first place. The last words of the novel summon up the "dream" of "Miklós Zrinyi, the poet," who, in "the old Zrinyiász," claimed that after his martyrdom angels had taken the spirit of his great-grandfather to heaven (II, 671).

With this closure Mikszáth pays homage to his predecessor, the author of the "old Zrinyiász," without admitting the relevance or validity of the religious framework which is its *raison d'être.* As I have briefly indicated at the outset of this discussion, Miklós Zrinyi, the poet, has taken a historical incident and has transformed it in accordance with the dictates of the Christian tradition. It is the Christian tradition that informs *Szigeti veszedelem,* and it is the Christian tradition that renders it meaningful. Implicit in the seventeenth-century epic is the Christ-like sacrifice.

In fact, Zrinyi's martyrdom in the old poem is even compatible with recent Christian interpretations of the parables. According to John Dominic Crossan, parables are "subversive" fictions which depend upon a reversal of the hearer's expectations. Thus, the story of the Good Samaritan is told in such a way that the hearer expects the Jew to help his fellow Jew, but it ends by showing that, in this instance at least, it is the non-Jew who has performed according to expectations. Thus, the hearer hears the opposite of what he has expected. This structure, according to Crossan, is central to Christianity and is applicable to Christ as well. When Christ dies on the cross, this seems to be the "judgment of God against Jesus, but, according to the Christian tradition, this death is really a triumph over death."[13] By the same token, the Zrinyi of *Szigeti veszedelem* dies the death of a martyr, but, according to the theme of the epic, his death is really a victory in that it permits the Turks to think of their temporary triumph as in some sense permanent when it is in fact the first sign of their ultimate defeat. Zrinyi's own death is, of course, a victory in the more conventional Christian sense as well: in dying out of this life, the self-sacrificing hero is born into the next.

Both the beginning and the ending of Mikszáth's novel allude to this religious framework. But while the beginning purports to be the record of a divine error, the end is a mere reference to the profoundly religious closure of *Szigeti veszedelem*. In other words, in no sense can the "religious framework" of the *Új Zrinyiász* be taken seriously. What is serious in *Szigeti veszedelem* is comic in Mikszáth's novel. And it is comic precisely by virtue of the comparison it invites the reader to make only to frustrate the grounds upon which that comparison may rest.

What conclusion can we draw from this explicitly elicited but implicitly rejected comparison? Certainly not merely that the religious fervor present and operative in the seventeenth century is absent and inoperative toward the end of the nineteenth. When with the closure of his novel Mikszáth returns his hero into the context which ends his predecessor's epic vision, he is performing an act that exceeds the dimensions of a failed comparison. Even as the Zrinyi of the seventeenth-century epic cannot find his place in the nineteenth-century novel, the nineteenth-century novel cannot dispense with him except by returning him to the context in which he belongs.

Notwithstanding his heroic past, the Zrinyi of the *Új Zrinyiász* is ultimately indistinguishable from a selfish scoundrel. This is not because he is different from what he was in the epic vision of his great-grandson, but because of the novelistic vision of the nineteenth century, which, in an attempt to remain true to the age of which it is an interpretative picture, cannot change the shallow context of its foreground. The modern Zrinyi becomes a scoundrel precisely because a "modern" Zrinyi is a contradiction in terms. Given the situation at the end of the nineteenth century, there cannot be a "modern" Zrinyi. Thus, the closure of the novel is in keeping with the integrity of its explicit theme, namely, that the Zrinyi of old is intrinsically incompatible with the modern world into which the novelist forces him to prove the very preconceived incompatibility which is the novel's paradoxical starting point.

CHAPTER 4

The Late Novels

I Különös házasság *(1900)*

ONE of Mikszáth's acknowledged masterpieces, *Különös házasság (Strange Marriage)* first appeared in book form in 1901. Since the plot of the story unfolds in the early decades of the nineteenth century, *Különös házasság* can be said to be a historical or at least a period novel.[1] It is essentially the chronicle of a failed marriage annulment, and, as such, it conjures up all the social forces, both the sacred and the secular, that play a significant role in the human drama which is the core of its plot.

The human drama involves three main characters with a whole gallery of supportive figures whose *raison d'être* is determined by the stance each takes with respect to the triangular conflict, both on the personal and on the social or public levels. The conflict arises when Count János Buttler, who is betrothed to Piroska Horváth, is forced into marriage with Baroness Mária Döry. This forced marriage is the way by which Mária's father, Baron Döry, intends to save the family honor. At the time of the forced marriage Mária is pregnant, and the father of her future child is none other than the parish priest. The forced marriage, then, is a means whereby a potential scandal is avoided; but since Buttler, who is in love with another, does not simply submit to his fate, the avoidance of one scandal is merely the creation of another, much larger one.

The legal contention that ensues, with its oppressively tedious progress, with its hopelessly political entanglements, with its crushing, self-interested, and face-saving maneuvers, comprises most of the remainder of the novel. According to one critic, *Különös házasság* is "not really about János Buttler's suit against Mária Döry. This is only the starting point of the real suit, the contention between the progressive and the reactionary, the democratic and the feudalistic, the age-old historical struggle between the light and the dark."[2] In following all the vicissitudes that pertain to this larger-than-life legal battle, Mikszáth's novel expands into a gigantic historic panorama in which the reform movement of the early nineteenth century struggles valiantly against the reactionary forces of the Church and of the royalistic establishment.

The Buttler-Döry suit is based on an actual marriage case responsible for a nationwide scandal in 1792. For purposes of his own, Mikszáth moves the case up to the 1810's. This way the valiant struggles of the incipient reform movement can enlarge the thematic preoccupations of the novel and add credence to the crushing battle between legal justice and moral defeat. In the actual case upon which *Különös házasság* is based, the idea of the "forced marriage" is itself a legal fiction used by Buttler's lawyers to effect the annulment of an estranged marriage. In Mikszáth's novel the forced marriage is *the* reality upon which the rest of the plot and its thematic unfolding is founded.[3]

Although the Catholic reaction to the novel's strong anticlerical stance was belated (only in the 1930's were there serious attempts to discredit the novel on the basis of its historical inaccuracies),[4] skeptical voices did make themselves heard at the time of the novel's serialization. Mikszáth responded to these voices with a note appended to the sixth installment of the novel by stating that "a story should always be true, if well told, but not in the sense of 'this is what happened,' rather, in the sense of 'this sort of thing can happen.' "[5] This note makes it clear that Mikszáth's interest is not in the historical truth behind his novel but in the large, thematic drift a version of that historic truth may suggest and allow to be developed along artistic lines. The novel, then, is neither to be credited nor discredited on the basis of its correspondence or lack of correspondence to history; it is to be judged solely as a work of art.

Furthermore, the reason why Mikszáth takes on this theme in 1900 is attributable to the fact that in the last decade of the nineteenth century reactionary, clerical forces gained ascendancy within the Liberal Party, a gain of which Mikszáth strongly disapproved.[6] *Különös házasság,* then, is a warning against the kind of forces that crush Buttler's happiness, not in 1792, but in the novelistic reality into which Mikszáth casts them where without a doubt, they are responsible for gross injustice in the paradoxical name of its opposite.

Notwithstanding its serious and highly controversial tone, *Különös házasság* has a happy ending. When Buttler's last and final appeal for the annulment of his "marriage" with Maria Döry is unsuccessful, the hero outsmarts the whole corrupt system by pretending to die. After his "death" he is finally able to take up with Piroska who has been faithfully waiting for him throughout the long and tedious years of the suit. This twist in the plot is characteristic of Mikszáth's novelistic solutions. I have already shown this special mixture between the Realistic and the Romantic in *Szent Péter esernyöje* and, to a different degree, in *Új Zrinyiász*. As in these earlier novels, in *Különös házasság*, too, this mixture between the Realistic and the Romantic is part and parcel of the novel's theme.

The implications of this theme are unmistakable. In the world of Mikszáth's novels corrupt, greedy forces constantly obstruct human happiness. The corrupt, or the greedy, is frequently associated with what is "real," with the way things are in the "real world," whereas what is humane, uplifting, and conducive to happiness is frequently associated with what is "fairy-talish," with what is poetic. The internal human capacity for making life beautiful is constantly up against the external human perversity for rendering men's existence less than tolerable. It will be clear that the theme of *Különös házasság* is a profoundly universal one, and Mikszáth's "fairy-talish" resolution of the novel's plot is an intricate part of that theme.

The structure of the story's emplotment and its narrative ploy, which is in some ways reminiscent of the reflexive technique used in *Két választás Magyarországon*, promote the thematic unfolding of the novel to the point where it can transcend both the historic framework upon which it is based and the contemporary developments against which it is a warning. In this case the structure of the story's emplotment is a significant key to the novel's underlying meaning. The basic structure of the novel is built on a scheme of plot vs. counterplot. This twofold structure is introduced by the ground situation, then the conflict created by the ground situation is repeated in the series of legal contentions that follow it until, finally, Buttler's ultimate counterplot revokes the validity of the original plot set in motion in the beginning of the novel by Maria Döry's father. A more detailed look at the events that compose the novel will clarify not only this construction but its underlying meaning as well.

As the novel opens, Buttler and his friend, Zsiga Bernáth, are on their way home from school. Buttler, who is an orphan, resides at the Bernáth household. During a stopover in their homeward journey, the students enjoy the hospitality of the Döry family. It is at this point that Baron Döry learns of his daughter's illicit affair with the parish priest, and it is at this point that the plot whereby his daughter may be saved from a devastating scandal occurs to him. Mikszáth's narrator, however, does not take the reader into his confidence. In other words, the reader is continually slightly behind the plot of the novel. It is always in retrospect that certain aspects of the parts of the story already narrated assume their full significance.

Once the hint of the Döry plot is dropped, the narrator begins to elaborate upon the counterplot of the ground situation, that is to say, the narrator establishes that aspect of the story which goes against the likelihood of Buttler's agreeing to become Mária's husband. Even as the background of the Döry plot is full of sinister innuendoes, Buttler's idyllic love for Piroska Horváth is full of the stuff of which fairy tales are made. By means of a flashback the narrator recounts the story of Master Horváth along with the story of the seed of love which is to grow between Buttler and Piroska but which is not to be harvested till well after the long and arduous delay of the hopeless legal contention that is to come.

Master Horváth, the lovable eccentric, corresponds with Buttler in the name of his daughter for a period of five years. During this time the protective father comes to know the character of his prospective son-in-law well enough to rest assured that his favorite daughter would be in honorable hands if she married Buttler. When, during this fatal visit from school, Buttler musters up enough courage to ask for Piroska's hand in marriage, he also learns the true identity of his former correspondent. Since Piroska has been in love with Buttler from the beginning anyway, this strange and unusual revelation does not present an impediment as far as the young couple's future happiness is concerned. The engagement takes place, and Buttler is ready to return to school for a final term.

On their way back from their vacation, having been previously invited, Buttler and Bernáth once again stop over at the Döry estate. At this point Baron Döry's insidious plot is ready to engulf Buttler's eagerly anticipated happiness with Piroska. There are many signs at the Döry household which indicate that things are not what they should be, but the innocent youths have no reason to suspect foul play. They take the strange occurrences (such as the three armed men who await them on the road to escort them to the Döry estate, or the fact that, once there, they get rooms in distant parts of the mansion) in their stride. By the time Döry makes a completely unexpected offer of his daughter to Buttler, it is too late. The unwilling youth is forced, at gunpoint, to marry the dishonored Mária. To rub salt into the wound, the marriage ceremony is performed by the very priest who had previously seduced the "bride." During the night, when the "bridegroom" finally falls asleep out of sheer mortification, a sense of utter helplessness, and exhaustion, his room is hoisted up, by means of a previously built mechanism, to form part of the bride's bedroom. In this way "witnesses" will later be able to testify that they found the new couple together the morning after their wedding night.

The marriage ceremony over, and apparently "consummated," Buttler is free to go. He is, at this point, fully confident that this invalid marriage will be quickly annulled. In fact, at this point in the plot, confidence in the law and in its ability to swiftly deliver justice never wavers. It is not until two legal masterminds are called in by István Fáy—Buttler's guardian—that the scheme of plot vs. counterplot is repeated for the second time.

One of the legal masterminds, Buttler's former professor, is an idealist who is certain that the outrage perpetrated upon Buttler will be swiftly redressed. It is the second legal mastermind, the incurable realist, who introduces the first note of doubt. He predicts that the Döry faction will produce "witnesses" who will testify to the fact that everything concerning the Buttler-Döry wedding has gone according to expectations. With this prediction the theme of legal justice vs. moral justice is fully launched. This theme will now be in the forefront of almost the entire remainder of the novel.

The theme of legal justice vs. moral justice is itself built upon a twofold structure. That is to say, implicit in the novel's unfolding of its plot is the practical theme of legalistic face-saving for the sake of protecting appearances, as well as the more theoretical, even philosophical, theme according to which in the eyes of the law truth and falsehood are structurally indistinguishable from one another. The first note of this second, theoretical or philosophical framework, is sounded by the realistic legal mastermind when he states that the " 'truth [of Buttler's case] is beside the point' " (III, 203). The validity of the lawyer's observation comes home to the reader with a vengeance when at the beginning of the long delayed hearings both

Buttler and his "wife" give their testimony. Since the members of the canonical tribunal are not in the privileged position of the reader, that is, since they do not in fact know that the marriage in question *was* actually a forced marriage, the "countess's" testimony sounds just as plausible as that of her justifiably outraged "husband." So long as the truth is not known with any degree of certitude, the judges remain in a position to see the possibility of the truth or falsity of either side. Truth, in other words, is not self-evident. The words of falsehood may sound true even as the words of truth may sound false.

Given this implicit theoretical framework, the more practical theme of legalistic face-saving in order to protect appearances, in order to maintain the illusion that legal justice *is* moral justice, can easily tilt the scales against the latter. If the marriage is declared invalid, then the priest who performed it must also be declared to have profoundly misued, even abused, his power. Since the priest is a representative of the Church as a whole, his act of perfidy will taint the entire clergy. It is this realization that tends to undermine the cause of truth and justice. In other words, given the possibility that a falsehood may *appear* to be the truth (and *vice versa*), whichever appearance is more beneficial for the maintenance of the illusion that legal justice *is* moral justice will be the one opted for by the judges. And this is precisely what happens. At one point the powers-that-be declare that this " 'marriage case must be handled with a *great deal of discretion*' . . . Ah, this discretion," the narrator adds, "in our land it is always under the foot of justice" (III, 262, italics and ellipses Mikszáth's).

Once the first tribunal declares the "marriage" to be valid, all further appeals seem doomed from the start. The progressive forces that rally behind the Buttler faction are incapable of reversing the judgment. Buttler's tremendous wealth, of which he spares little to further his cause, is also powerless to tilt the scales in favor of moral justice. When, at the point of death, one of Döry's false witnesses confesses to having committed perjury, Döry hires other witnesses who testify that the repentant "witness" was not in her right mind. And so it goes on. Every time the Buttler faction is permitted the luxury of renewed hope, the Döry faction counters their moves with still more false witnesses who continue to allow the legal system to abide by its previous decision with a clear conscience.

Meanwhile years go by. Master Horváth is killed in a duel by

Döry. This is another instance of falsehood winning over truth. When, during his testimony, Döry implies that the whole marriage case is Horváth's insidious ploy to save Buttler's fortune for *his* daughter, Piroska's father is forced to resort to a duel to save the appearance (in this case also the substance) of his honor. In the end all fails. When Buttler's wealth succeeds in planting a priest sympathetic to the hero's cause in a high position within the Church, the new archbishop also betrays Buttler by turning his back upon the truth. His words to Buttler well summarize the novel's stance on the issue of legal justice vs. moral justice:

> "What you demand of me, my dear count, is absolutely impossible. This cause is no longer yours alone. Your share in it is but a trifle; it is hardly visible. This has been a tremendous battle, my dear count, waged between the Church and those elements that look askance upon the clergy. It is very sad indeed that the battleship we were obliged to sink carried your wheat as part of its cargo, but sink it we had to, as it also carried our enemies, who would have shipwrecked our own vessel."
>
> (III, 346)

Within the world of *Különös házasság* legal justice consistently betrays moral justice. This seems paradoxical in that the purpose of legal justice is precisely the safeguarding of moral justice. By the law of averages alone, moral justice should have a fifty-fifty chance. And perhaps it does. But not in this novel.

Lest the novel seem perversely one-sided, it should be borne in mind that the story explores the vicissitudes of but a single case. Another case may have fared better, even in the hands of the same judges. Buttler's case had the support of the truth, but appearances were against it. And, as the novel rightly implies, appearances are powerful indeed, inside or outside of Mikszáth's vision.

Yet, notwithstanding the inexorable impetus of its plot, *Különös házasság* has a happy ending. This is possible because legal justice is not the sole safeguard of moral justice. There is also poetic justice, both the poetic justice represented by the Romantic, fairy-talish aspects within the novel and the poetic justice of the novelist himself. The dark world of legal justice, then, with its false commitment to appearances, does not exhaust the world of *Különös házasság*. There is room in it for the light world of a poetic vision which illumines the better half of its interior landscape, and which permits the true lovers to escape from the clutches of the powerful forces that would keep them apart. The lovers accomplish this, in the end, by outwitting these same powerful forces.

The Romantic aspects of the novel do not discredit its heavy-handed Realistic ones. The two exist side by side; neither is influenced or tainted by the other. The one is perversely evil, the other incurably good. Yet it is the Romantic vision that defeats the Realistic forces, even if by default only. During the long years of trial and error, Buttler and Piroska approach one another at times just to be near one another. Although Buttler is forced by a hastily granted promise never to see Piroska during the course of the trial, like the hero of some fairy tale he disguises himself as a gardener just to be near his sweetheart. Later Piroska performs a similar trick when she disguises herself as a maid just to be able to clean her beloved's rooms. The plot that successfully counters Döry's initial plot is also the plot of a fairy tale. In the end Buttler gives almost all of his wealth away to various charities (the sole proviso in his will is that no Catholic priest ever benefit by them, which proves that, heroic as he is, Buttler is very capable of a humanizing grudge) after which he journeys to Vienna where he conveniently "dies" of a heart attack.

Lest the strongly anticlerical stance of the novel be misunderstood, it should be pointed out that there is an implicit distinction throughout between human justice on the one hand, and divine justice on the other. At Buttler's "funeral" this distinction becomes explicit. When his "widow" comes to pay her last respects, Bernáth, Buttler's lifelong friend, questions her right to be there. When she replies that she is, after all, Buttler's wife, Bernáth's simple response is: " 'yes, according to the priests . . . but not according to God' " (III, 373). This, of course, is part and parcel of the Romantic vision which transcends, and thereby triumphs over, the Realistic one.

It should also be pointed out that poetic justice deals justly with Mária as well. It appears that Buttler's "wife" was hopelessly and desperately in love with her "husband." It is not difficult to imagine how unhappy her father's initial plot must have rendered her earthly existence. Her own daughter, the child born of her illicit affair with the priest, remains a grim reminder of her transgression throughout. In the end her long suffering humanizes her to the point where she even wins some of the reader's sympathy, and this makes her unrelieved suffering even more poignant.

The final chapter of the novel is highly Hawthornesque. It is a matter of common knowledge that Hawthorne's narrative technique frequently gives the illusion that the reader is free to choose between the various plausible interpretations of a given event or situation. At the end of *The Scarlet Letter*, for example, we are told that the reality of the Red "A" imprinted on the flesh of the Reverend Dimmesdale's bosom is questionable. Hawthorne's ploy is to imply that among the witnesses there were those who did and those who did not see it. Even those who saw it attributed different causes as to its appearance. Hawthorne's narrator lists these different interpretations and invites his readers to choose from among them whichever they like best. Yet the careful reader is not really free to choose. The narrator's words: "those best able to appreciate the minister's peculiar sensibility" usher the reader toward the one interpretation most in agreement with the thematic drift of the entire novel.

Mikszáth's handling of Buttler's "death" employs a similar narrative ploy. And this is in keeping with the narrative technique of the novel as a whole. Even as *Két választás Magyarországon* uses the fiction of reportage, *Különös házasság* utilizes the ploy of a chronicle. Rather, according to its opening sentence, the novel is really a kind of running commentary on another text: "I am writing these things *according to a chronicle*, the pages of which have not yet turned yellow, *exactly* as they follow" (III, 9, italics mine). Hereafter the narrator even claims to avoid all literary embellishments as these would tend to *add* to the truth of the story something that simply need not be added. The fiction of the chronicle is maintained throughout. The narrator's own commentary is usually clearly commentary, and it usually takes the form of outrage or disapproval. It does not, however, imply that anything in the story is his own interpretation of it. He is merely writing "according to a chronicle." The interpretations within the narrative are always the interpretations of various characters in it. Thus, even the notion that Mária may have been desperately in love with her "husband" is the interpretation of a particular character who insists that the idea is merely a whim of his (III, 322).

The final chapter of the novel, the crown of its Romantic undercurrent and the triumph of its poetic justice, is consistent with this narrative ploy of detachment. "They say," the narrator insists, and "this legend spread," he continues (III, 367 & 377). What do they say, and what legend spreads? Why, the legend that Buttler is not dead and that he lives happily with Piroska (who also disappears after the hero's funeral) in some other land. At the very end the narrator seems to put the legend into question by stating that "this belief persisted for a long time . . . but it never reached larger dimensions, which is indicated by the fact that [Buttler's] coffin (although there was talk of this) has never been opened" (III, 377).

At this juncture it may seem, then, that the legend is only a legend (and perhaps we should keep in mind that legend literally means: "to be read"). Earlier, however, the narrator does drop a hint that may well be a plausible explanation as to why the legend "never reached larger dimensions." The revolution of 1848 seems to have drowned out almost all memory of the entire Buttler affair (III, 376). If this is so, it also explains why the coffin has never been opened to verify the legend of Buttler's happy life with Piroska elsewhere. Furthermore, one person does open the coffin the day before the funeral. At that time, however, the narrator fails to inform us explicitly of what this faithful and loving servant sees. We are only told that he "dropped the lid of the coffin in panic" (III, 368), and that he wasted no time in having it hermetically sealed (III, 372). Later this faithful servant inexplicably informs another servant (under the guise of demanding utter secrecy) that what the coffin contained was a " 'wooden figure, properly dressed, placed in sand and shavings' " (III, 377).

The narrator's cautious disclaimers, then, amounted to no more than an implicit distinction between inside and outside information. Unlike the members of the tribunal who do not know the truth about Buttler's marriage, the reader is in a privileged position all along. Except for those immediately concerned, most characters within the novel are in the same situation as the members of the tribunal, that is, they do not have inside information either. But the reader does. And the same is true of the "legend." Most characters within the novel do not have the inside information the reader is privileged to possess.

This implicit distinction between inside information (shared by the reader and a few characters in the novel) and outside information (possessed by most of the characters in the novel) rounds off the basic structuring principle of the entire work, the scheme of plot vs. counterplot. Falsehood triumphs in the realm of the one; truth in the realm of the other.

Különös házasság is, in the final analysis, the inside narrative about an "outside" that vests everything in the realm of appearances (life as we think it is must go on), while it is also about itself, about its own poetic vision that penetrates the realm of appearances and thereby saves whatever it can of the substance (life as we know it is must nevertheless have a chance). So what the novel ultimately implies is that while its Realistic core (the judgment on Buttler's case) deals falsely with its charge, its legendary core rectifies that falsehood. The artistic truth of the novel implicitly gives the lie to the Realistic "truth" of its own counterpart.

II A szelistyei asszonyok *(1901)*

Although its tone and execution are typically Mikszáthian, *A szelistyei asszonyok (The Women of Szelistye)* is a Romantic novel-length anecdote reminiscent of the innumerable folktales built around the figure of King Mátyás the Just, the great Renaissance ruler of Hungary (reigned, 1458–90). The lore that has accumulated around this greatest of Hungarian kings is substantial, and Mikszáth's "novel" is a typical contribution to it.

The causes of Mátyás's unprecedented popularity (of Hungary's national heroes only Prince Rákoczy II [1705–11] and Lajos Kossuth, Governor of Hungary [1849], can rival him), are not difficult to locate. During his reign the country made tremendous advances in the political as well as in the social spheres, and after his death Hungary was never again a significant European power, a land completely independent of vexing foreign interference. In fact, it would not be an exaggeration to state that after Mátyás's death the tragic history of this small Middle European nation is a series of uninterrupted footnotes to a chronicle of gradual national decline. What had captured the imagination of the people, however, is the king's legendary righteousness, his uncompromising sense of justice, and his indubitable honesty and fair play.

"Only Once Was There a Dog Market in Buda"—the origin of which, according to internal evidence, is close to the conception of Mikszáth's novel—is a good example of the Mátyás lore. It recounts the story of a cruel farmer who takes sadistic delight in the shortchanging of the downtrodden and the poor. He once tells an impoverished fellow villager that King Mátyás is buying dogs for substantial sums of money. The poor peasant sells his sole cow to be able to purchase dogs. He then journeys with his newly acquired pack to the royal court in Buda only to find that he has been made a fool of. When his pitiful wailing reaches the ear of the King, Mátyás gives him a sympathetic audience and ends by paying a fabulous sum for the poor man's dogs. The cruel farmer, upon learning of this unbelievably fortuitous sale, also sells most of his property in order to invest his ready cash in dogs. He, too, journeys to Buda, hoping to make a highly advantageous business transaction with the King. His "joke" upon the poor peasant, however, turns back upon him, for King Mátyás, realizing who the farmer is, tells him mischievously that "only once was there a dog market in Buda."[7]

A szelistyei asszonyok, both in its tone and in its execution, partakes of this legendary Mátyás lore. Unlike in *Beszterce ostroma, Szent Péter esernyöje, Új Zrinyiász*, or *Különös házasság*, however, Mikszáth makes no attempt here to compare the old with the new, the Romantic with the Realistic, or the legendary with the mundane. *A szelistyei asszonyok* is nevertheless a substantial work. Although critical reception has relegated it to a relatively minor position in the Mikszáth canon, its thematic preoccupation with the role of play-acting and the confidence game of fiction-making in the realm of the real, its insight into the imaginative alterations the mind makes in the fabric of the actual, into what the world is and how the creative spirit transforms it according to the contours of its own desires, lifts it well above the level of the "lighter, more weightless [realm of the] operetta," as one critic has classified it.[8] It would be truer to say, along with a more recent critic, that in works such as *A szelistyei asszonyok*, Mikszáth's treatment of historical or semihistorical data is deliberately "ahistorical," that the "demythologizing intent" is everywhere manifest in them. Although Mikszáth does "link the events [of such novels] to great historic personalities . . . what he seek[s] in them is a humanity similar to our own."[9] Instead of the grandeur of the past, which more often than not is merely the invention of the shallow, nostalgia-ridden present, Mikszáth tries to show the genuine grandeur present in the commonplaces of the past. His *Szelistyei asszonyok* is a good case in point.

The plot of the novel receives its impetus from a delegation of Wallachian women, from the remote Transylvanian village of Szelistye, to a representative of King Mátyás. The women submit that since they have contributed all of their men to the King's army, they are now forced to live without the many benefits provided by the opposite sex. They demand that the King send them men to replace the sons and husbands sacrificed to the King's cause. The governor who hears their complaint makes an official promise, in the name of the King, to fulfill the women's desire. The remainder of the novel is the amusing chronicle of the fulfillment of this official pledge. Since both the request and the promise are highly unusual and unprecedented, and since more pressing demands upon the King's attention frequently intervene, the final fulfilling of the Wallachian women's desire is not without obstacles and vexing delays.

The plot of how the women of Szelistye get their men is worked out with the utmost care and credibility. Notwithstanding Mátyás's legendary sense for justice and fair play, the powers of bureaucracy Mikszáth attributes even to the simpler art of government of the fifteenth century, and the—at times—debilitating confidence games Mikszáth never denies the humanity that populates the pages of his works, are the causes of the delays.

The first obstacle is posed by the imprisonment of the governor who makes the pledge in the first place. When the ledger book containing the governor's official promises to various groups finally reaches the King, Mátyás takes immediate notice of the unusual promise made to the women of Szelistye. Now that the King knows of the pledge, and now that he is not disinclined to make it good, another obstacle rears its head. One of Mátyás's nobles who has seen the women in question happens to remark that they are not exactly beautiful. The wise and just king thinks of this as a rather important factor. Since the only practical means by which the wishes of the women of Szelistye may be granted is the sending of an assortment of ex-mercenaries and disabled veterans, the King's question is, would it not be unjust to repay them for their military services by relocating them with a group of " 'ugly witches and Xantippes' " (III, 393).

With this twist in the plot comes the confidence game that reopens the issue and that does, finally, get the desired results. The women in question happen to be the serfs of a powerful nobleman whose profits, due to the same lack of men the women of Szelistye have complained of, have dwindled significantly. It would, therefore, be in his interest as well to have the King fulfill the pledge originally made by the now disfavored governor. But this is not the only consideration that puts the whole question in a different light. The women's desire for men can be, and is in fact, interpreted in a variety of conflicting ways. Part of public opinion (especially its feminine part) sees the desire of the women of Szelistye as ungodly and sinful. There is another faction that counters this view by pointing out that the women need the men to till the soil, that they need the men, in short, because their very livelihood depends on them. There is also the point made by the women themselves, namely that without men how will they ever be able to produce future soldiers for the King's army? When another nobleman in the royal circle remarks that the women of Szelistye are not after all so ugly as to constitute the punishment of the ex-soldiers who may be fated to wed them, the King's solution is to ask for a "sample" of the maids and widows who reside in the village in order to make his final determination.

At this point the Transylvanian nobleman assigns one of his underlings the task of locating three beautiful women (one blond, one brunette, and one with black hair) to make up the "sample" requested by the King. The underling succeeds in this enterprise admirably. The women are found, and with various bribes and other tantalizing promises, they are made residents of Szelistye (for the nobleman's sense of verisimilitude is strong). Word is sent to Buda that the "sample" is ready for the King's inspection.

When the women arrive at the royal court, the King happens to be "vacationing" at one of his Transdanubian estates. And here another complication is added to the plot. The owner of the inn where the women decide to sojourn in Buda falls in love with the single Wallachian maid among them (the other women are widows and not Wallachian) and his feeling is reciprocated. By the time Mátyás sends escorts for the women from his Transdanubian estate, the innkeeper arranges with the women's Transylvanian chaperone to accompany the group disguised as a coachman. The chaperone, being a kind man, agrees, and thus the maze of deceptions slowly multiplies. First, the women are not really representative samples of the women of Szelistye (in fact, they are not really from Szelistye at all), and second, one of them is not even looking for a husband any more as she is already betrothed to an innkeeper who will now pretend to be a coachman.

The next deception is planned by the King himself. Now that the youthful Mátyás knows that the delegation from Szelistye is on its way to his Transdanubian estate, he has an additional problem. Since he is "vacationing" with a retinue of riotous young noblemen, and since he knows that his cronies are not above taking undue advantage of the fiasco about to materialize, and since he also knows that his own royal intentions remain honorable with respect to the original demand made by the women of Szelistye, he has to find a way of carrying this whole affair off with the appropriate flair it intrinsically suggests, but without any undue aspersions it may potentially bring in its wake.

In order to keep everything within the well-established boundaries of due propriety, Mátyás opts for a bit of playful confidence game of his own. He decides that his fool will take on the role of the king and that his servants will assume the roles of his nobles. He and his real nobles will, in turn, play the servants. This way the "king" and his "retinue" will not misbehave since they will have to operate in the full view of the real king and of his real retinue, while at the same time the real king and the real retinue, as "servants," will not be able to permit themselves the luxury of taking advantage of the women (this would jar with the verisimilitude demanded by the success of the game) who come before them in good faith. Furthermore, if the "servants" do indulge in a bit of innocent hanky-panky, and if word gets out about this, the improprieties will be attributed to the servants and not to the royal retinue (III, 398).

The King's wise and clever scheme goes according to plan, but not without further twists and complications in the plot. As the honest innkeeper, who is reasonably protective of his new bride, attempts to bribe one of the "king's" honest-looking "servants" (the real king), Mátyás learns the truth about the "sample" from Szelistye. The innkeeper's words that " 'nothing is true in one of these royal palaces, not even the fact that I am a coachman,' " contain, of course, even more truth than their speaker realizes (III, 440).

Although the real king now knows of the attempt that has been made to deceive him, he does allow the fiasco to continue a little longer. But not without testing the innkeeper's character and not without presenting him with a riddle whereby the innkeeper may guess the full import of his own words that " 'nothing is true in one of these royal palaces.' " Mátyás sends the innkeeper some mediocre wine in a golden decanter and some excellent wine in an ordinary clay container with the message that "*these two jugs exemplify the situation*" at the estate (III, 447, italics Mikszáth's). I mention these fine details of the plot as they continuously indicate the kind of thinking attributed to the king in the rich Mátyás lore of which Mikszáth's novel is an accurate representative.

The "royal show" ends with each of the women choosing a gift to remember the occasion by, as well as a husband as a forerunner of the King's intention to fulfill his promise to the women of Szelistye. The King, of course, intervenes in a relatively unobtrusive way to make certain that the Wallachian maid is able to choose the innkeeper for her husband. One of the widows, however, chooses the King himself, and this creates quite a commotion, but just at that moment a portion of Mátyás's army arrives with three hundred prisoners of war. The real king now puts an end to the proceedings by revealing his true identity. The women's choices are honored, and the appropriate weddings follow in due course; all except one. The widow who has chosen the King himself merely becomes his mistress.

The wishes of the women of Szelistye are now also on the verge of being fulfilled. But Mátyás's sense of justice will not permit the deception his Transylvanian nobleman had attempted to perpetrate upon him to pass without some appropriate punishment. Along with the prisoners of war, he sends word to his powerful underling that he will shortly visit Szelistye and that if the women are not as beautiful there as the "sample" would indicate, the nobleman will lose his head. So it comes about that the Transylvanian nobleman exchanges all of the women of Szelistye (who thus find husbands for themselves elsewhere) for some of the most beautiful women in the world who duly become the wives of the happy prisoners of war. Mátyás's more pressing involvements in matters of state, of course, keep him from ever visiting Szelistye, and it is much later in his life that he hears about the legendary beauty of the women there.

What raises this novel well above the level of entertainment is its implicit metafictional import. I have already commented on a variety of the configurations of this theme in the earlier sections of this book, and I shall discuss its significance at some length in the chapter that follows this one, but there is still room here for a few words about the contribution this particular novel makes to this overall preoccupation. As the foregoing discussion of the plot of *Szelistyei asszonyok* indicates, the structure of the novel is built around a twofold deception.

First, there is the attempt to create the fiction that the women of Szelistye are all beautiful, and second, there is the King's own "show" to mislead the Transylvanian delegation into thinking that what is not, is. Both these attempts are deliberately deceptive, both try to form an appearance intended to be mistaken for a reality. Both, however, operate from honorable motives. The women of Szelistye really deserve new husbands to replace the ones they have lost in the King's wars, and the delegation from Transylvania does deserve the King's protective ploy by means of which the propriety of the whole affair may be safeguarded. The only person whose motives are tainted in the entire plot is the nobleman whose interests in obtaining men for the women of Szelistye are clearly monetary. But the King's threat is not only an adequate punishment for this unsavory self-interest, it also assures beautiful wives for the men whose lives, even though they are prisoners of war, are rather arbitrarily arranged.

Both of the deceptive plots, then, are ultimately such that they make the lives out of which they grow and into which they bring a harvest of sorts richer and more appealing than they would otherwise have been. Both of the deceptive plots are, in fact, examples of the kind of creative tampering with the fabric of reality I mentioned earlier in this discussion. By pitting them against one another, by making them intermingle with one another, and by revealing each to the other while each is still in full swing (the innkeeper's confession to the "servant" and the King's riddle about the decanters that "exemplify the situation" are the central manifestations of this), Mikszáth succeeds in illuminating this human tendency of shaping the forces constantly at work in real life as well as in the life of fiction. By creating the creation of appearances intended to be mistaken for realities, *Szelistyei asszonyok* becomes a metaphor, literally a "carry-over" from real life into fiction in such a way as to be also the guarantor of the reader's return from the fiction into real life. Implicit in the artistic truth of the novel is the truth of the extraartistic tendency that gives birth to art in the first place.

III Akli Miklós *(1903)*

Akli Miklós (Miklós Akli), like *A szelistyei asszonyok,* is a fanciful romance the plot of which unfolds within the broad confines of a historical era. As the subtitle of the novel, "the History of the Imperial Entertainer," indicates, this tale is also intricately connected with an actual ruler. Here, however, we are not in the glorious Renaissance, but in the equally controversial age of the Napoleonic Wars. Akli is the official fool of Francis I (reigned, 1798–1835),

Emperor of Austria, whose daughter, Maria Lujza, was to become Napoleon's second wife. As in the previous novel, here, too, the historical forces at work in the novel (in this case the first decade of the nineteenth century) are kept at bay. They form the backdrop of a somewhat demythologizing tale which, in recounting the fortunes and misfortunes of the "imperial entertainer," show us as much of the common life of the era as its fanciful, Romantic preoccupations allow.

The story concentrates on Miklós Akli's early days as Francis's royal fool, on his growing romance with the Emperor's "adopted" daughter—Ilona Kovács—, on his fall from royal grace, on his unjust imprisonment, and on his final return to the royal court to obtain Ilona's hand in marriage. Even this brief outline of the novel's plot should be an adequate indication of the potential contrast between the Realistic and the Romantic the reader frequently encounters in Mikszáth's works. The thematic uses to which this contrast is put here are somewhat reminiscent of the theme of legal justice vs. moral justice running through *Különös házasság*. Here, however, Mikszáth's satiric rays are not focused on the intrinsic problems generated by the very existence of legality per se, but rather on malicious, behind-the-scenes machinations that rest upon the fundamental recognition that a lie is structurally indistinguishable from the truth.

At the outset of the novel, Mikszáth introduces another structuring principle, the myth of the wise fool. Like that of the sad clown, the myth of the wise fool can easily be sentimentalized, but Mikszáth avoids this potential flaw in *Akli Miklós* by the satiric use to which he puts it. This satiric element is present at the beginning of the novel and remains throughout as a kind of steady undercurrent. The Emperor's love for Akli is the subject of many rumors, but in the final analysis none of them reflect disfavorably on the court since, as the narrator remarks, the public knows that their ruler is better off with a man "who pretends to be a fool than with those who simulate wisdom" (III, 509).

But, as the myth of the wise fool demands, the cause of Akli's fortune is also the cause of his misfortune. Count Stadion (another actual historical figure), one of the Emperor's advisers, quickly learns to dislike Akli who, in an attempt to keep the Emperor well entertained, frequently succeeds in making the Count look foolish. The Count begins to search for a plot for Akli's downfall. This is no easy enterprise since the Emperor appears to love Akli dearly. The substance of the Count's eventual case against Akli appears early in the novel, but it is not developed until much later. Akli, who is (among other things) skillful with the pen, writes a Latin poem which foretells Napoleon's victory. This can be construed as treason.

After this hint of Akli's future undoing, Mikszáth turns the plot back to the atmosphere of its initial felicity. The seed of malice is planted, but its eventual ability to sprout is apparently not taken into consideration. At this point the story turns to a typically Mikszáthian idyllic development in which there soon arises a Romantic conflict. Earlier in the story a Hungarian colonel inadvertently sacrifices his life for Francis I when he becomes the mistaken target of a would-be assassin. Francis semiofficially, and under a great deal of secrecy, "adopts" the colonel's orphans (György and Ilona Kovács), and appoints Akli as their apparent guardian. As Ilona grows into a beautiful young lady, an unconfessed love develops between the girl and her apparent guardian. At this point Count Szepessy, an eccentric nobleman, comes to Akli for an audience. It should be mentioned that one of the Emperor's favorite sources of entertainment is to eavesdrop on these "audiences." Count Szepessy (whose eccentricity issues from his unwillingness to dress according to his station in life) demands Ilona's hand in marriage. When he is about to shoot Akli, who refuses to divulge the identity of Ilona's true guardian, the Emperor reveals himself.

Since the eccentric nobleman may well be a likely candidate for the hand of the Emperor's charge, Francis decides to use Akli as a go-between between Ilona and her suitor. If the girl is not against the marriage, the Emperor would not disapprove of the match either. What Akli's conference with Ilona reveals is that the girl reciprocates her guardian's secret feelings for her. As the young lovers dilly-dally in the idyllic setting of a public park immediately in the felicitous aftermath of their newly made proclamations of love, two secret policemen approach and arrest the surprised Akli.

Akli is imprisoned in Vienna without ever learning of the charges against him. Immediately upon the arrest Ilona rushes to the Emperor to clarify what appears to be some bizarre misunderstanding. The benign Francis is about to act in Akli's behalf when Count Stadion shows up with the pro-Napoleonic poem, the evidence of Akli's treason. Ilona never learns why the Emperor is suddenly adamant on the whole Akli question.

At this point the reader is not much better off than Ilona herself.

The causes of the plot against Akli are evident, but their seriousness is at first highly questionable. The poem, reproduced in Latin as well as in translation earlier in the novel, is clearly pro-Napoleonic, but it is a private manuscript never intended for publication, the political import of which also seems to fall short of the Emperor's unmistakable fury. Count Stadion's argument, however, is that the pro-Napoleonic poem is probably a sign that Akli is a spy. Akli's trial will, therefore, depend on the secret police's ability to dig up some more tangible evidence for the royal fool's treachery. This argument convinces the Emperor and with it, the theme of legal justice vs. moral justice enters the plot (more of this later). Since such evidence is not forthcoming, Akli stagnates in prison. When György Kovács succeeds in smuggling a letter out from Akli's prison and manages to get it into the hands of the Emperor, the scheme meets with a failure that worsens Akli's situation. Akli is sent to prison in Hungary, and this also ends the secret correspondence he has been able to keep up with Ilona.

The eventual unraveling of the spuriousness of the charges against Akli is also the unmasking of the myth of the wise fool. Around Christmas one day, after Akli has already been stagnating in prison for a number of years, the Emperor decides to test György's knowledge of Latin. It so happens that Akli's pro-Napoleonic poem is used for the test. György explains to the Emperor that he is familiar with the poem, as Akli has written it specifically for him as an example of the kind of versification that reads one way when read forward and another way when read backward. Read forward, the poem is a prophecy of Napoleon's victory; read backward, on the other hand, its meaning is the opposite, a warning to Napoleon that all his military victories will lead to ultimate defeat. Count Stadion's interpretation, whereby the poem is a sign of Akli's secret political ambitions, is now seen as a foolish misinterpretation the cause of which is Akli's excessive wisdom. Akli, who is wiser than those around him, thus becomes the victim of his own wit. His wit is what causes Stadion to turn against him in the first place, and an example of his wit is what permits Stadion to offer highly circumstantial but nevertheless plausible evidence of his treachery. Akli's misfortune, in fact, is the embodiment of Henry David Thoreau's remark that "sometimes we are inclined to class those who are once-and-a-half witted with the half-witted, because we appreciate only a third part of their wit."

Akli is, of course, immediately released from prison and requested to return to Vienna. On his journey back, however, he uncovers a plot that seems to threaten the very happiness he is now in a position to anticipate. What Akli learns is that Count Szepessy is on his way to Vienna with an "army" of three hundred nobles with whose aid he intends to abduct Ilona from the school for young ladies from which she is about to graduate. Akli sends a letter of warning to the Emperor, but the message is intercepted by one of Szepessy's men. The "army" is moving toward Vienna in small groups in order to avoid the suspicion of foul play. Akli manages to join up with the "insurgents." Although he has no reason to believe that the Emperor will not receive the letter of warning, he cannot absent himself from Szepessy's men for he hopes that were something to go wrong, he would still be able to intervene at the opportune moment to save Ilona from her fate.

Szepessy's plot is worked out with great care. The "army" intends to congregate around the school for young ladies late Christmas night when the whole city is asleep and when the police is not likely to be on the alert. The plan goes admirably until the very last minute. When word is sent to the principal of the finishing school that unless Ilona Kovács is immediately released she will be removed by force, the young ladies resort to what appears to be an ingenious counterplot. They are seen taking pieces of furniture to the school's attic which they apparently intend to ignite so that the ensuing fire may alarm the neighborhood and bring the authorities upon the "insurgents."

Akli's own counterplot, however, makes the one devised by the young ladies unnecessary. Akli reveals himself to Szepessy and informs the count that Ilona Kovács is really Maria Lujza and that the "switch" has been made in order to save the real Habsburg girl from marrying Napoleon. Upon hearing this, the Count immediately abandons his plans for the abduction, and Akli appears to be in a position to marry the girl of his choice at long last. On the day of the wedding, however, Szepessy attempts to assassinate Akli whose recuperation thus produces a final delay before his happiness can be realized.

Akli Miklós abounds in the use of numerous scripts the varying interpretabilities of which play a significant role in the novel's thematic unfolding. I have already shown how Akli's apparently pro-Napoleonic poem is utilized to be a central turning point in the novel. It is clear how its false, that is, incomplete interpretation puts

Akli in prison, and how its true, that is, complete interpretation is responsible for his liberation from prison. This movement from the incorrect to the correct interpretation of a script is repeated in Akli's fiction that Ilona is really Maria Lujza, but with a difference. In one of the novel's early episodes, where Akli is to take some fresh fruit to Ilona, the Emperor gives his fool a slip of paper with which he may prove to the gardener's wife that he is acting on the Emperor's orders. The slip of paper says: "This one time Akli is telling the truth. Francis I" (III, 525). This little joke proves useful to Akli when he invents the fiction of the "switch." He produces the faded slip of paper for Szepessy's benefit, and this lends incontestable credence to his tale. Akli uses the words: "This one time Akli is telling the truth," for the sake of verifying a lie, and the ploy works.

By means of these variously interpretable scripts, Mikszáth adds to the fundamental theme of the structural indistinguishability between a truth and a lie. And this theme blends in well with the other theme that pervades the novel, the theme of legal justice vs. moral justice. What the intricacies of the plot of *Akli Miklós* reveal is that it is an illusion to think that the legal system, which has been devised for the sake of safeguarding moral justice in the first place, always accomplishes its purpose. One of the narrator's early remarks is an explicit indication of the way in which this illusion may be undermined: "the power of a belief . . . is greater than that of a fact" (III, 509). The plausibility of an interpretation is what gives support to the interpreter's belief that he has penetrated to a truth. But, as *Akli Miklós* frequently makes it clear, plausibility is no guarantee of correctness. Plausibility is built upon the interpreter's ability to think logically, but, as the narrator remarks elsewhere in the novel, "logic is nothing but a pretty mental exercise with which a man may deceive the less gifted and sometimes himself as well" (III, 623).

In the world of *Akli Miklós*, then, man seems to be hopelessly vulnerable to mistaking lies for truths, appearances for realities, and *vice versa*. The very end of the novel, however, is a good case in point for Mikszáth's way out of this dilemma. After Szepessy's attempt to assassinate Akli, the Emperor calls off the wedding because of the superstitious fear that God himself may be against it. The trouble is that there is a "legend" afoot according to which the Maria Lujza, who is to marry Napoleon, is really not Maria Lujza. The fact that Akli is not allowed to wed Ilona after all (whom the public fancies to be the "real" Maria Lujza), seems to give credence to what the public cannot help suspecting: that this whole thing is some sinister plot to keep the Habsburg girl out of Napoleon's reach. In order to dispel these rumors, the Emperor is forced to permit the marriage between Ilona and his former fool.

According to narratorial claim, these final episodes of the novel are based on the published "memoirs" of the sexton of the church where the wedding takes place. As this sort of narratorial claim is usually self-reflexive (it brings attention to itself as a transparently fictional ploy to add mock credence to the truth of the narrative within which it occurs), by its use Mikszáth makes an implicit distinction between self-conscious and unself-conscious interpretations. Interpretations which are aware of the vulnerability of their own logic are self-conscious whereas interpretations that fancy their logic to be invulnerable are unself-conscious. The former may or may not be true, but the possibility of their error is always self-evident. The same is not true with respect to unself-conscious interpretations. Since these are unaware of the vulnerable logic upon which they rest, they trust blindly in the conclusions they reach.

According to the world of *Akli Miklós,* blind trust is what renders even the best-intentioned legal system to occasionally betray the moral justice it is trying to safeguard. It is only by making the behavior of his narrator deliberately transparent that Mikszáth can bring the reader's attention to this distinction, and it is only by means of this distinction that the profound philosophical undercurrent of the novel can agitate the surface where the direction of that undercurrent must become perceptible.

IV A vén gazember *(1904)*

Of all of Mikszáth's novels discussed so far in this book, *A vén gazember (The Old Scoundrel),* first published in book form in 1906, is closest in its structure to an extended folktale. As folktale, it follows the basic myth of the impoverished "princess" who finds riches and happiness by wedding a "hero" rising from the masses. But this is an oversimplification for, by following this basic structure, *A vén gazember* is also a tale which specifically addresses itself to the myth of class distinctions, more particularly to the distinction of inherent as opposed to inherited nobility.

The novel chronicles the story of two generations. The first is separated by the notion of inherited nobility which, by virtue of inherent nobility, is fused with the second, while in the second generation the class distinction itself breaks down and ceases to be the divider of its respective members. The starting contrast in the first generation is provided by Baron Inokay and Gáspár Borly, his steward. Gáspár Borly is known as the "old scoundrel," for it is believed that as the Inokay family is slowly deprived of its wealth, the steward is gradually accumulating his own by highly dishonest or at least unsavory means. Meanwhile László Borly, the steward's grandson, falls in love with Inokay's daughter, Baroness Mária Inokay, and—class distinctions notwithstanding in the long run—his feeling is reciprocated.

When Borly, the old scoundrel, dies, his last will and testament reveals that rather than enriching himself at the expense of the Inokays, he has devoted his life to saving the family fortune for the sake of Mária and Pál, her brother. The Baron, who now realizes that all his life he has been falsely maligning his saintly steward, refuses to accept the "inheritance." The problem posed by this act of nobility is eventually resolved by Mária's marriage to László Borly.

Basic to the plot of this novel is the myth of the virtue of disobedience. This myth is familiar to English readers in that it plays a prominent role in the "late" Shakespeare. In fact, three of the so-called "serene romances," *Pericles, Cymbeline,* and *The Winter's Tale,* turn upon the act of a disobedient servant who, by virtue of his disobedience, is actually responsible for the happy outcome of these plays. In *Winter's Tale,* for example, Leontes, King of Sicilia, in a fit of jealous rage suspects that his infant daughter is not really his. He orders his faithful servant, Antigonus, to take "his" offspring to a forsaken place and there murder her. Antigonus, however, disobeys this order and lets the child live. Because of this act of disobedience, as well as because of a previous act of disobedience by another servant, this drama, which could easily have turned out tragically, ends up as a serene comedy.

Intrinsic to the myth of the disobedient servant is the notion of moral responsibility it entails. The servant is loyal to his master and as such is to be obedient to all of his wishes. When the master's wishes, however, go against his own welfare, the servant must be capable of making the independent moral judgment which will manifest his authentic loyalty by taking the master's welfare rather than the master's immediate orders as his ultimate guide. In this way, by disobeying his master the servant is in actuality obeying the dictates of his master's best interests.

By the time the story opens, the wealth of the Inokay family is dangerously depleted. This depletion is attributed to Steward Borly, the "old scoundrel," whereas it soon becomes clear for the reader that Baron Inokay is a prodigal, nonproductive nobleman who thinks more of the honor involved in paying up gambling debts than of the possible virtue of frugal living. This is, of course, the real reason why the family fortune has slowly but surely dwindled away and not old Borly's behind-the-scenes deals which, as it later turns out, save and increase much of the family's fortune. This information, however, is well guarded from the reader for the most part of the novel.

The reader is, in fact, in a slightly aprivileged position in that he knows no more of the truth about the "old scoundrel" than do the characters inside the novel. The careful reader can, however, detect a curious discrepancy between old Borly's reputation and his kindly, albeit eccentric disposition toward all living things, including lame dogs. His eccentricity is best evidenced by his apparently convoluted reasoning in indenturing his smarter grandson, László, to a locksmith, while providing the funds for the higher education of his less gifted grandson, István. Borly's eccentric reasoning is that a priest need not be smart since the Church's power will form a protective shield around him, but that a locksmith needs all the wits he has been endowed with if he is to survive and succeed in the competitive world of the journeymen.

Borly's decision to indenture László widens the social gap between the boy and his "sweetheart," the Baroness. While László is learning the art of his trade, Mária is being educated in a nearby convent. László visits her in secret, and it is at this point in the story that the children's enterprising ambitions enter into the plot of the novel. The old-fashioned world where social mobility is highly limited, where the future of children is arranged for by parents and guardians, is here challenged by Mária's remark that worldly opinion would never permit her to become the wife of a locksmith but that were László to become an officer in the army, the situation may be more favorable to their eventual marrying. László runs away to Buda, joins the army, and his heroic acts soon assure him of a succession of promotions. Thus, by taking his career into his own hands, László is consciously preparing the way toward the narrowing of the social gap that separates him from the Baroness.

Meanwhile, the fortune of the Inokay family is fast diminishing. Inokay's friends try to persuade the Baron to run for political office, but the old prodigal and riotous ways of the nobility immobilize the Baron's willy-nilly ambitions; Inokay would still rather increase his fortune by the more "honorable" means of gambling. Old Borly, as a result of one of his many loyal acts to enhance the Baron's political chances, contracts pneumonia and dies.

László returns for the funeral, and old Borly's last will and testament seems to restore the Inokay family's honor. Inokay, however, is touched by Old Borly's innate nobility and, as a nobleman himself, feels it incumbent upon him to reciprocate in kind. He refuses to accept the "inheritance" on the basis of moral justice. Inokay is convinced that the wealth should go to the Borly children in that it is thanks to Old Borly's frugality and his shrewd investments that the money has survived and increased. Inokay feels that had he remained in possession of the money in question, he would have wasted it just as he has wasted the other portions of his estate.

Legal justice, of course, immediately rises to the occasion and threatens to thwart its moral counterpart. As the executioner of Borly's last will and testament explains, Baron Inokay has no right to refuse the "inheritance" in the name of his children (the actual heirs according to the will), while László has no right to refuse the refusal, first because he is not of age and, second, because he is not entitled to make such a move without the consent of his absent brother, István. This unexpected but perhaps not unanticipated conflict between impulsive nobility and cautious legality is resolved by László's betrothal to Baroness Mária Inokay. Thus the class distinctions which permeate the novel are transcended by the forces of the authentically human, and the novel ends on an irresistible note of optimism.

The surface theme of the triumph of Romantic idealism over Realistic cynicism, versions of which the reader has already encountered in a number of Mikszáth's earlier novels, is, once again, buttressed by an ingeniously constructed metafictional substructure. The idyllic story of *A vén gazember* not only chronicles the reversal of appearance and reality by showing how the "scoundrel" in life becomes a virtual "saint" after death, it also chronicles the playful reversal between fiction and real life by bringing strategic attention to its own novelistic unfolding.

When László and Mária first discuss the possibility of their eventual marriage, Mária informs the young apprentice that her friends highly disapprove of the alliance. Mária's own response to this disapproval, as she herself explains, is to pose the question: " 'are not novels [in fact] full of this sort of thing?' " The answer to this query is that while " 'novels [do indeed] abound in wonders, this sort of thing has never happened [in real life] and never will' " (III, 711).

Again, when László—anticipating his inheritance—thinks of refusing it himself, he also thinks of the fact that this would be the kind of "asininity which only happens in novels, and, furthermore, it would not even lead to [the desired] goal. This sort of thing only succeeds in novels because the novelist, in inventing one asininity, that of the refusal of wealth, quickly adds another whereby he [for whose sake the sacrifice is made in the first place] is deeply touched by the gesture" (III, 791).

What Mikszáth's characters do not find realistically acceptable, Mikszáth's novel unabashedly incorporates into itself as its own solution. Thus, the sort of thing that can only happen in novels comes to actually happen in this novel, too, but almost as if in opposition to the level-headedness of the characters who ultimately benefit by its happening. *A vén gazember*, then, makes an implicit distinction between real life, where justice does not triumph and happiness does not result, and life depicted in fiction by painting a picture of life where things go not according to the conventions of the "reasonable," but according to the conventions of the Romantic, the fairy-talish. The novel is, in this sense, a dream of a better world aware of its own status of dreamhood; and, by putting into the mouths of its dream-figures the distinction between fiction and reality, it is also aware of the possibility that it may awaken at any moment and find that the dream has after all come true.

V A Noszty fiú esete Tóth Marival *(1906–07)*

The second of Mikszáth's acknowledged masterpieces, *A Noszty fiú esete Tóth Marival (The Noszty Boy's Affair with Mari Tóth)* first appeared in book form in 1908. The core of the novel is based on a well-publicized event, one version of which can be found in the July

21, 1901 issue of *Nagyváradi Napló (Nagyvarad Diary)*, written by Endre Ady, the soon to be controversial poet:

> You have probably read about old Ungár's affair. He is a hard old Jew from Bácska, a millionaire, by the way, and the father of a beautiful daughter. Old Ungár's daughter has eloped with a shabby man, a twenty-year-old gentry boy. The loving couple had gone as far as Vienna and probably had a good time on the road. Further, however, they could not go. The old man intercepted them and rescued his daughter. The young eloper's decrepit relatives then surrounded old Ungár: "Nothing short of marriage can rectify this," [they said]. At the same time they now condescended to be friendly with the "insolently rich Jew" whom they had despised thus far. The old man then announced the date of the wedding. The proud gentry kinfolk came by the scores, for—on account of the millions—they were ready to accept the bride, mixed marriage and all. When the glamorous wedding party was all together, the hard old man also appeared on the scene and—having cast his daughter's silk dress in front of them—said, in his peasant-like manner, approximately this: "I am not willing to restore the gentry [honor] with my millions. My daughter has gone abroad. The gate is open . . ." It is unfortunate that this affair had been publicized. It was old Ungár's private business. But since it had been mentioned, it should also be stated that old Ungár is a hard man, but a smart man, too.[10]

Implicit in the Ungár affair is the conflict between the sober, commonsense values of the middle class and the extravagant, formality-ridden world of the gentry. With the 1905 elections and with the heavy losses suffered by the Liberal Party, this conflict assumed nationwide proportions. The Opposition, hiding behind patriotic zeal, turned to the traditional counties for support and, in the name of national independence, launched programs that but thinly disguised its own narrow class interests. It is under the pressure of this political atmosphere that Mikszáth began to write his *Noszty fiú*.[11]

The plot of the novel utilizes the political aspirations of the impoverished gentry class and shows, rather successfully, that its true motives were intricately bound up with its attempts to gain financial security for the sake of continuing its obsolete, extravagant way of life. The conflict between the opposing forces in Mikszáth's novel is concretized by Pál Noszty's irresponsible self-interests in the name of the historical minor nobility and Mihály Tóth's newly emerging middle-class values in the name of capitalistic free enterprise. Pál

Noszty and his kind operate by investing their respectable names in dishonest political gambles and shrewd behind-the-scenes machinations for financial gain, while Mihály Tóth relies on his own abilities and on his own honest labors and investments to grow toward financial independence and a humanistically acceptable existence.

The novel's unfolding story utilizes these opposing factions by showing how Ferenc Noszty's whole family joins forces to assure the young man's success in obtaining Mari Tóth's hand in marriage as well as by showing how this fortune-hunting plot meets with ultimate failure as it runs aground on Mihály Tóth's uncompromising honesty and commonsensical indifference toward empty formalities and shallow appearances.

The narrative mode of the novel (which is said to be the closest Mikszáth came to so-called Critical Realism) is somewhat reminiscent of the reportage employed in *Két választás Magyarországon*, but with a significant difference. Here the narratorial ploy is to shy away from the fiction of self-conscious reportage and rely, instead, on a straightforward, "gossip-like representationalism which puts on the mask of [informal] speech."[12] The narrator of *Noszty fiú* is, in fact, close to the ideally effaced author of post-Jamesian Realism. He does not write with explicitly acknowledged sources before him, nor does he bring attention to his own act of writing, except occasionally, and then by implying the existence of various sources rather than by specifically naming them. The gossipy formula of "they say," or "members of the Noszty family maintain," crops up again and again, especially in the earlier parts of the book (IV, 48, 52, 63, & 494), while an occasional allusion to or mention of a newspaper article can also suddenly confront the reader with an air of implied verisimilitude (IV, 472).

In his "Afterword" to the novel, Mikszáth openly admits that the narrative mode of *Noszty fiú* is consciously experimental and indicates that the novel of the future will rely less and less on arbitrary literary conventions while moving closer and closer "toward journalistic *reporting*." But, Mikszáth hastens to add, the art of the novelist will have to "ennoble the report, even as it had previously ennobled storytelling" (IV, 510, italics Mikszáth's).

Notwithstanding its admittedly experimental mode and its carefully maintained application of the above-mentioned narrative strategy, *Noszty fiú* still reads like a typically Mikszáthian achievement. As it will be clear, it relies heavily on certain Romantic conventions; it does not shy away from the anecdote-like episodes made familiar by the earlier novels, and it can even indulge in the idyllic, particularly when it comes to the treatment of love. Yet *Noszty fiú* is nevertheless a new departure for Mikszáth. The anecdote-like episodes play a less prominent role here than in his previous novels, and its idyllic parts are more often than not ephemeral or aborted.

The plot of the entire novel is unfolded by blocks where, in the words of the "Afterword," the "reporter relays to us the raw materials [of which the novel is composed], while parading before us the primary and secondary figures who participate in [the novel's events] without providing us with more information concerning their lives than is necessary for an understanding of the [novel's specific] occurrences" (IV, 511). In this way the telling of the story follows the inexorable logic of sequentiality.

Once the plot of the novel is launched by showing Ferenc Noszty's extravagant and prodigal life as a hussar officer, the rest follows almost as if by logical necessity. Whenever the plot reaches a point where background information becomes essential for the reader's continued understanding of all the intricacies of the grand fortune-hunting scheme which is the novel's core, the narrator unobtrusively fills in the necessary details. Thus the novel moves forward by emplotting the blocks of causes and effects that first lead to apparent success on the part of the Noszty clan, then to certain failure.

The Noszty plot to obtain a large fortune by means of marriage is undermined first by Mihály Tóth's discoveries concerning the true character of his prospective son-in-law, then by his counterplotting the second Noszty plot, the plot of compromising Mari Tóth's honor to the point where only the sanctity of marriage may be able to save it. Mihály Tóth, however, proves unwilling to sacrifice his daughter's happiness on the altar of appearances. His ploy to *appear* to give in to the barren formalities of the gentry class is a masterful stroke which not only ends the major conflict sustained throughout the entire novel, but which is in itself an impassioned plea for common sense and reason in the face of ever rising corruption under the mask of decency and apparent social cohesion.

At the time the story opens, the inexorable law of cause and effect is also launched, not to be impeded until the unsuccessful outcome of the devious Noszty plot to land a fortune by means of a matrimonial alliance. Ferenc Noszty is a dashing hussar officer in a small town where he is paying court to Rozália Velkovics, the mayor's daughter. His incorrigible gambling and generally irresponsible life-style soon get him into debt. His rival for Rozália, a sober and colorless business man, lends him money by having him forge the signature of his colonel on a promissory note.

When the allotted time runs out, Ferenc writes to his father for assistance. Noszty senior arrives with Ferenc's sister, Vilma. Baron Koperecky, the executive of a local bank, comes up with the money by demanding Vilma as collateral. By the time Ferenc rushes with the money to his rival's business establishment, the allotted time has run out (by a matter of half an hour or so), and the hussar officer has already been exposed to his colonel. Although the colonel is quickly reimbursed, Ferenc is forced to resign his officer's commission under the pretext of ill health.

Once the initial situation establishes the Noszty way of life, the rest of the plot can move forward by means of one thing leading to another. When the allotted time on Baron Koperecky's loan runs out, he claims Vilma's hand in marriage. What appeared to be a joke initially (Vilma being used for collateral) turns out to have been a sly little plot on Koperecky's part to win the Noszty girl for his wife. This plot is successful, but instead of a traditional dowry, Koperecky is rewarded with a political office. Vilma is, therefore, the first sacrifice on the altar of gentry irresponsibility.

It is at this point in the story that Mihály Tóth returns from America with his millions. As will be clear later, the fact that Mikszáth has his major spokesman grow rich in experiences as well as financially in America is itself of some significance. Democratic ideals together with the practice of free enterprise provide Mr. Tóth (he is frequently referred to as "Mister" in the Hungarian original) with the wherewithal to fight the political and moral corruption largely propagated by the gentry class of turn-of-the-century Hungary.

Mr. Tóth's predisposition to be beneficially influenced by America is clear from the beginning of his story. When he first comes into the capital with which he will later grow rich in the New World, he expresses his desire to settle in a land where " 'nobility is not necessary,' " where " 'there has never been a king' " (IV, 216 & 217). Mikszáth needs Tóth's American experiences to make later developments in the novel credible.

According to one of his critics, the figure of Tóth represents the ideal *citoyen*, the responsible spokesman of the interests of the middle classes. Since the bourgeoisie that played such a prominent role in Western Europe as well as in America after the French Revolution never flourished in Hungary, where this role is generally assumed by the minor nobility, the influx of Western European and especially of American ideals is necessary to combat the world of appearances upon which the entire Noszty plot is based.[13] For the Noszty plot is so ingeniously interwoven with the social order of turn-of-the-century Hungary that its failure is practically inconceivable. It is only Tóth's inexorable will to bring the best of the New World into the old that enables him to see through the world of appearances and to dispense with the social pressures it would otherwise exert even upon him.

Ferenc Noszty's idea to wed a fortune is actually his father's. Since the boy is good looking, this seems like a reasonable "career." When Mari Tóth is selected as a likely candidate, and when Ferenc begins to take an interest in the idea, Noszty senior remarks characteristically that he is glad that the " 'boy is finally looking to something [worthwhile]' " (IV, 160). Once Mari Tóth is selected as a likely candidate, the entire Noszty family pitches in to help Ferenc with his endeavor. It is up to Aunt Amália, the family "psychologist," to mastermind the plot. She researches Mari's weaknesses and provides Ferenc with the blueprint that will surely lead to success. It appears that one of Mari's major weaknesses is the notion that every suitor is after her money. Having been inundated with sentimental German novels, Mari is of a rather Romantic disposition. This prepares her for the "artificially manufactured romance" Ferenc will enact for her on the basis of Aunt Amália's hypothetical model (IV, 134).

Aunt Amália's hypothetical case is the following: Ferenc is to meet Mari, say, on a train, where he is to cast amorous glances at her. Having taken a careful note of Mari's appearance, he is then to advertise in the personal columns of various papers the Tóth family subscribes to that he is searching for a maid of such and such appearance, last seen on such and such a train, whose beauty has quite enchanted him, etc. This would not only feed into Mari's Romantic predisposition, but it would also allay her fears that suitable young men are merely interested in her money. Ferenc accepts Aunt Amália's blueprint wholeheartedly and introduces one of the many metaphors used throughout to evoke the Noszty plot. He states that he will follow Aunt Amália's plan as would a " 'soldier who is fighting a war' " (IV, 186).

The opportunity to act upon this blueprint soon presents itself when the Tóth family decides to vacation in a well-known wine-producing region in Transdanubia. Ferenc disguises himself as a hunter and waits for developments that will enable him to go through with the first act of his plot. Mari's Romantic predisposition once again plays into his hands. In an attempt to find out whether or not she is attractive to members of the opposite sex, Mari changes clothing with her maid in order to attend a local dance given for the tradesmen of the region. It is here that the first meeting between Ferenc and Mari takes place; it is here that the "artificially manufactured romance" begins. It should be noted that while both participants are consciously enacting roles designed to hide their true identities, Mari is acting innocently, merely in accordance with her Romantic predisposition, while Ferenc's moves are calculated and preconceived. Mari's ulterior motives amount to a foible, Ferenc's to a vice.

When Rozália Velkovics appears on the scene (she happens to be Mari's first cousin), Ferenc mysteriously disappears. This development, too, appears to play into the fortune hunter's hands. The false idyll is a total success. Mari is completely taken in by the mysterious hunter who appears to respond to her as she would be without her riches. Ferenc's next step is to wait and to advertise in the personal columns of strategically selected papers. Now it is the Noszty family's business to provide Ferenc with a political office in the region where the Tóth estates are located.

After a certain time Ferenc and Mari meet again, this time in their real persons. Ferenc now simulates disappointment. He tells Mari that since she is the daughter of a millionaire the gap is now greater between them than it was before, for while it would be conceivable for a Noszty to marry a mere maid (after all novels are full of this sort of thing), how can he aspire to be anything more to her now than a loving friend (IV, 371, 374).

Mr. Tóth, however, is not so much after a good "match" as he is after his daughter's happiness. The one thing that matters to him is the character of Mari's would-be bridegroom. Ferenc appears to be the kind of man who would make his daughter happy; therefore, Mr. Tóth does not discourage his suit. When the young man shows

Mari the advertisements he had placed in a number of papers as proof of his past attempts to find her, the gamble appears to be won.

At this point Velkovics, Rozália's father and Mr. Tóth's lifelong friend, falls seriously ill. This necessitates Mr. Tóth's absence just at the time when Ferenc's suit is ready to reach its anticipated climax, the desired engagement. Mikszáth's narrator does not go into details here, but it is clear that Mr. Tóth learns enough about young Noszty's character to turn back the tide of his spectacular rise. Not only does Mr. Tóth know Rozália's father (the truth about Ferenc's former suit of Rozália damages him in Mari's eyes), he also knows the colonel whose signature Ferenc forged on that promissory note of long ago. Upon Mr. Tóth's return, when Baron Koperecky is ready to make a formal request for Mari's hand in marriage on behalf of his brother-in-law, the well-designed Noszty plot appears to meet with failure.

It is here that the ruling formalities of the day begin to enter the picture. Ferenc's first impulse is to challenge Mr. Tóth to a duel for defamation of character. The situation, however, is unique, and the formalities of the case remain ambiguous. It is, after all, permissible for a father to reject a suit. The question is, *why* has Mr. Tóth *changed* his mind? It *appears* that he has learned something about Ferenc's character and this entitles the young man to "demand an explanation" (IV, 431).

This ploy is soon abandoned when Aunt Amália comes up with a second plot, the execution of which seems to guarantee success. This second plot is more dishonorable than the first in that it entails more than an "artificially manufactured romance." Once more the Noszty family will join forces, this time to abduct Mari in order to compromise her to the point where only marriage can save the *appearance* of her honor (it should be noted here that her *real* honor will never be violated).

The Noszty family now decides to put on a theatrical performance the benefits of which will go to a suitable charity. Mari is asked to participate in this enterprise. On the night of the dress rehearsal things go "wrong," all in accordance with the Noszty plan. A bridge is closed for repairs on Baron Koperecky's orders; Mari is forced to spend the night in his father's hospital; Ferenc shows up there disguised as an old watchmaker, and so on. In the end, Ferenc sneaks into Mari's room where he manages to persuade her of his innocence (what has weighed more with Mari than anything else was Ferenc's previous suit of Rozália). The following morning the young couple is discovered (it should be mentioned that Mari agrees to this part of the plot), and it appears that the marriage will be forthcoming after all.

Mr. Tóth would still be willing to go through with the marriage, but now he begins to suspect the whole love affair has been insidiously designed to entrap his daughter. It is at this point that the big battle between appearances and common sense begins. When, after the "scandal," Mr. Tóth receives a formal request for his daughter's hand, formalities seem to take the upper hand. Mrs. Tóth's ambitions combined with her pride do, however, challenge Mr. Tóth's adamant refusal to give in for the sake of appearances. Mr. Tóth, satisfied with the knowledge that Mari would not want to marry Ferenc if she knew for certain that the whole affair had been the well-designed plot of a clever fortune hunter, runs into a serious stumbling block in the person of his own wife. Mrs. Tóth's pride plays such a prominent role here that the pressure it exerts almost undermines her husband's firm resolve not to sacrifice his daughter on the altar of appearances.

The social pressures alone weigh heavily on Mr. Tóth's shoulders. All his friends advise him to give his daugher to the Noszty boy to "repair" the damages caused by his having "compromised" Mari. Tóth responds to all arguments with the force of irresistible logic. If his daughter has indeed lost some of her "market" value by having been thus compromised, would it not be truthful to say that the traditional reparation by marriage would devalue her even more? For if the person who has compromised her was unworthy of her to begin with (otherwise the compromise would not have been necessary in the first place), would her value not diminish even more by marrying the person in question? When Mr. Tóth's friends prove unable to refute these arguments, they invoke the final trump in their hand: the sanctity of tradition. Mr. Tóth will still not give in. " 'It may be the custom, but it is a bad custom,' " he replies. Why should " 'parental duties be based on vanities and external considerations in the preparation of a child's future?' " (IV, 480–83). Mr. Tóth, convinced that his principles are founded upon reason, fares well with his friends.

His wife, however, proves to be a more obstinate obstacle. Her response to his arguments is simply that he is " 'overly confident of [his] own reasoning. But there are men who are smarter than [he] is' " (IV, 488). Here Mrs. Tóth resorts to all the cliches Mr. Tóth has heard already, and this seems to indicate that the millionaire's wife is totally enslaved by the world of appearances. The element of her pride, however, soon modifies this picture. If Mr. Tóth refuses to give his daugher to the Noszty boy, in the eyes of the world the Noszty family will be the winner. Even if the papers were to expose the insidious Noszty plot, people may still choose to disbelieve the facts and trust in the appearances which do not place the Tóth family in a favorable light.

When Mrs. Tóth actually attempts to end her life, Mr. Tóth's reserves are finally broken down. He now devises a masterful counterplot that will allow for appearances but will not allow them to swallow the substance. He *apparently* agrees to the wedding, but by the time the Noszty clan arrives in pompous formal glory, the bride is no longer in the vicinity. Mihály Tóth's final speech to the Nosztys is a masterful triumph over appearances by means of appearances: " 'You, Ferenc Noszty, have dealt such a low blow at my girl that I was forced to obtain for her the satisfaction that the appearance of your relatives here will provide. I am sincerely sorry and I apologize for having dragged them here under false pretenses, but I was obliged to relieve my child of the shame which after all that has happened would have made it seem that the [Noszty] family was unwilling to accept her. There are probably some *gentlemen* among you, my dear sirs, who will appreciate [my predicament]' " (IV, 505).

Noszty fiú is Mikszáth's great novel of manners which is at the same time the great novel against manners. The historical roots of the conflict upon which the novel turns have already been mentioned. The part the minor nobility played in the political changes that followed the 1905 elections is undoubtedly the starting point of Mikszáth's interest in turning the well-publicized Ungár affair into a full-length novel. Once the novel gets under way, however, the forces that set it in motion become somewhat subservient to the larger theme of appearance vs. reality. In order to make this theme deliver what it is capable of delivering, Mikszáth produces a novel in which the mixture between the Romantic and the Realistic plays an integral part.

It is frequently maintained that the Romantic elements flaw this otherwise Realistic masterpiece.[14] This sort of argument seems to lead to a theoretical confusion between the novelistic illusion of reality and the thematic exposure of the illusions that operate in real life. It is precisely by making Mihály Tóth, for example, an idealized *citoyen* that Mikszáth can make him credible within the context of the novel's general argument. The novel clearly takes issue with the common practice of sacrificing the substance for the sake of saving the appearance. In order to formulate an adequately conceptualized counterforce capable of convincingly triumphing over the empty formalities that dominate the social life of turn-of-the-century Hungary, Mikszáth has to represent not so much the reality as the idea of the kind of thinking that can successfully achieve this end. In the real world, too, the idea would have to precede the reality. In this sense *Noszty fiú* is not a Realistic novel; that is, it is not a merely accurate description of life as it is perceived by the mythical average man, but an apparently Realistic concretization of a thesis, namely, that appearances should never be permitted to sacrifice the substance.

Of further implications inherent in Mikszáth's continued practice of mixing the Romantic with the Realistic I shall say more in the chapter that follows this one. Let it suffice to say here that what appears to be a flaw in *Noszty fiú* as a Realistic novel is precisely what enables it to deliver its theme. The conventions of fiction can never be removed from conventional fiction. The very attempt to do so would either be a self-evident contradiction in terms or an example of the writer's ability to delude himself or his readers. It is one thing to point this out, however, and quite another to remember that while it is not possible to remove all conventions from conventional fiction, it is possible to hide them, to keep them out of the reader's immediate focus. As he explains in his "Afterword," Mikszáth does take the trouble to remove some of the more blatant and arbitrary conventions from his storytelling, but in doing so he introduces a new convention, that of reporting, which is still admittedly in the service of artistic rather than of mere Realistic truth.

VI A fekete város *(1908–10)*

Mikszáth's last novel, *A fekete város (The Black City)*, the third of his acknowledged masterpieces, first appeared in book form posthumously in 1911. As a result of its author's untimely death, the novel suffers somewhat from the lack of revision other serialized works had undergone prior to their appearance in book form. Like

Különös házasság, this novel is also written against the vast panorama of a significant historic era, but here the real historic forces remain in the background while the novel's own "history" is allowed to dominate the foreground almost completely.

The plot of the novel is taken from the lore of the Görgei family, more specifically from István Görgei's work, "A Görgei nemzetség története" ("The History of the Görgei Genealogy"), which recounts the deputy sheriff of Szepes County's murder of the judge of Löcse, of the City of Löcse's intent to revenge itself upon the deputy sheriff of the county, and of the ultimate success of the city's vengeful enterprise.[15] Mikszáth adds little to this basic plot. The deputy sheriff's murder of the judge begins the story, and the city's vengeance on the deputy sheriff ends it. Packed in between is the story of the failed idyllic love between Görgei's daughter, Rozália, and Antal Fabricius, the young judge of Löcse (and the third in succession from the murdered one), who successfully carries out the vengeance without realizing that Rozália is Görgei's daughter, thus, without realizing that by advancing the cause of "justice" he is at the same time, irreparably destroying his own future happiness with Rozália.

The conflict between Pál Görgei, the deputy sheriff of Szepes County, and the City of Löcse, more specifically the City Council of Löcse, is not without a certain symbolic value, especially if we see it against the historic backdrop of the great *kuruc-labanc* conflict in the last third of the seventeenth and the first decade of the eighteenth century. The *kuruc* (the term derives from the Latin *crux,* meaning cross) were the followers of Imre Thököly and later of Prince Ferenc Ráckoczy II (leader of the anti-Austrian insurrection, 1705–11), and they were composed, for the most part, of impoverished serfs and of the Hungarian nobility. They fought heroically for liberty and for national independence in the immediate aftermath of the Turkish occupation which had lasted for well over a century. Ráckoczy II envisioned an independent Hungary and for this end he even sought, ultimately unsuccessfully, an alliance with the Sun King, Louis XIV of France.

The *kuruc,* consisting of irregular "armies" and mainly preoccupied with guerilla warfare, frequently engaged the *labanc* (nickname of the pro-German mercenaries who fought on the side of the Emperor of Austria), at times with considerable success. Although with the defeats of 1708 and 1710 the *kuruc* insurrection ended, the military losses were not followed by total political failures. The achievements of the Ráckoczy era heralded the Period of Reconstruction during which the "grievous wounds of the Turkish era were healed."[16]

The conflict between Görgei (the county) and the authorities of Löcse (the city) corresponds, to a certain degree, to the *kuruc-labanc* contest in that the county represents the Hungarian nobility while the city stands for the foreign element (the burghers of Löcse were, for the most part, German Saxons). Lest this quasisymbolic parallelism be misunderstood, it should be pointed out that in *A fekete város* Löcse remains, at least on the surface, sympathetic to the *kuruc* cause throughout.

In another sense, however, the conflict between the county and the city is contrasted unfavorably with the great historic backdrop against which it unfolds. It is almost as though Mikszáth were saying that while the entire nation is bleeding for the momentous cause of liberty and independence, the petty conflict between Görgei and the City Council of Löcse is a futile loss of time and energy which represents a tragic inability to transcend minor quarrels in the face of all-consuming, historically significant causes. The irony present throughout the novel in the contrast between the petty and the local, on the one hand, and the grand and the national, on the other, reaches universal proportions; particularly as it becomes an implicit debunking of the idealization of the past.

While the historians (especially the academic historians) of the Hungarian millenium (celebrated in 1896) saw the heroic eras of the past as totally committed to the ideals prevalent in their time, Mikszáth's method of contrasting the local with the national at the expense of the local and at considerable loss for the national, is an attempt to demythologize the past. As *A fekete város* clearly indicates, in reality it is entirely possible for great historic moments to turn awry because of petty, local considerations. Alongside the heroic and the grand there flourishes the unheroic and the miniscule. For every giant step in the history of a nation, there are the innumerable minute steps that lead nowhere. In the world of the real as opposed to the world of the idealized past, great national tragedies may well go unheeded, while personal and local ones may tragically upset the lives of those immediately concerned.

Despite this contrast between the macrocosmic and the microcosmic, mostly at the expense of the latter, the microcosmic itself assumes universal significance as the plot of the novel unfolds. The opening section of the novel is devoted to the characterization of Pál Görgei.

Görgei is a temperamental nobleman whose wife's death in childbirth causes him unspeakable suffering. His tiny daughter, Rozália, is taken over by his brother's family, and when their daughter—born approximately at the same time as Rozália—dies, Görgei becomes the victim of a self-generated suspicion. He thinks that his brother, out of the goodness of his heart, has exchanged the dead baby ("really" Rozália) with the living child, figuring that two deaths in rapid succession would be too much for Görgei to bear. The secret anguish that Görgei suffers as a result of this unwarranted but nobly inspired suspicion is aggravated by his inability to find some conclusive proof to the contrary. He knows that his suspicion may well be a false inference drawn from the nobility of heart he attributes to his brother, yet he is still unable to shake it off.

Görgei is also aware of the dangers inherent in his quick temper. For this reason, in his capacity as deputy sheriff of the county, he tries not to pass judgment on various delinquents except at times when he is unusually calm and collected. He constantly thwarts his tendency to flare up by heroic attempts at self-control. It is nevertheless his quick temper that gets him into trouble with the City of Löcse by compelling him to "kill" its judge. When during a hunt in winter the judge of Löcse shoots Görgei's dog while attempting to hit a rabbit, the enraged deputy sheriff fires upon the judge, exclaiming, " 'a dog for a dog' " (V. 92). This is the episode that sets the plot of the novel in motion, and it is the final resolution of the conflict created by this episode that ends it, with the beheading of Pál Görgei on the orders of the City Council of Löcse.

Görgei's act is certainly rash and unwarranted, but this does not change the fact that the City of Löcse is even more despicably in the wrong. Nustkorb, a city official and a member of the judge's retinue at the time of the incident, decides to carry the wounded judge into Görgei territory where an area encircled by the blood of the dying judge (according to an ancient royal edict) will be legally annexed by the City of Löcse. The greed and the cruel indifference with which this despicable act of land acquisition is carried out puts Görgei's rash act into a new and highly mitigating perspective. Rather than heed the pitiful supplications of the dying judge, the members of the City Council of Löcse go so far as to press the bleeding wound to squeeze every last drop of blood out of it in order to increase the land area to be annexed by the city. In a sense, then, it is the members of the City Council of Löcse who are their judge's real murderers. And their act is not mitigated by a noble, albeit sudden and unwarranted, act of passion; on the contrary, they act with coldly and indifferently calculated foresight motivated by greed.

The city's reaction to this incident is mixed. The public is outraged by Görgei's act, but some members of the city council are also shocked by Nustkorb's as well. Nustkorb defends himself on the basis that he has acted in the city's best interests. His logic is highly convoluted. He claims that the now dead judge would himself have wanted it this way (the reader knows that the dying judge certainly did not), and he also claims that the judge had frequently maintained in various speeches that he would gladly " 'offer his last drop of blood for the growth of the city' " (V, 111). As convoluted as Nustkorb's defense is, it does help to win the favorable opinion of most members of the council. One subsequent speaker goes so far as to argue that, although Nustkorb's act may go " 'against certain of God's laws,' " no one can deny that there is " 'some value in it in accordance with the laws of the city.' " It also goes without saying, this same speaker continues, that " 'we are here to represent the city and not God . . . whatever troubles [therefore] Nustkorb may have with God, let him settle with God . . . [while] as far as we are concerned, who are merely the city's representatives,' " we must side with Nustkorb (V, 113).

With this distinction between divine justice, on the one hand, and human justice on the other, Mikszáth draws an admirably clear picture of the forces behind the county (rash, irresponsible nobility) and the forces behind the city (cold, opportunistic "bourgeoisie"). This picture is the exact reverse of the one presented in *Noszty fiú* where it is the corrupt gentry's greed that compares unfavorably with the values of the middle class as embodied in Mihály Tóth. Notwithstanding their cold and calculating nature, the burghers of Löcse are also capable of rash acts. This is evidenced by their decision to order the entire population of the city to wear black (thus the novel's title) as a sign of mourning until such time as the city will effect the revenge for the atrocity enacted upon its judge by the deputy sheriff of the county.

For much of the remainder of the novel, during which the conflict between the county and the city remains at a standstill, Mikszáth meanders back and forth between various subplots (with occasional hints at the historic struggle between the *kuruc* and the *labanc*). Of major importance is the subplot involving the idyllic love that grows between the Saxon Antal Fabricius and Görgei's daughter Rozália. Once Rozália is well into her adolescence, Görgei decides to send her to the finishing school at Löcse. Her true identity will, of course, remain a well-guarded secret. One of the most colorful characters in the novel (one of Mikszáth's many interesting "eccentrics"), a man who leads a double life by dividing his time between residence at Löcse and the "occupation" of a Turkish pasha with a private harem, is entrusted with Rozália's "guardianship."

When this "guardian" is on his way with Rozália Otrokócsy (her alias) to the Löcse finishing school for young ladies, Antal Fabricius first meets her under highly Romantic circumstances. The episode involves highwaymen and an impromptu feast at the christening of a miller's newly born son. As is customary with Mikszáth, the lovers' idyll is impregnated with the Romantic atmosphere of fairy tales. But, as in many of the previously discussed novels, this Romantic atmosphere is not extraneous to the book's essential theme. Unlike in *Szent Péter esernyöje*, however, where the conflict between the Romantic and the Realistic (love and greed) is most similar to the same conflict in *A fekete város*, here the poetic (love) does not triumph over the prosaic (greed, among other things); here love does not overwhelm the forces which wittingly and unwittingly conspire against it.

For the relatively long period of time during which Rozália grows up and, later, lives at Löcse in carefully guarded secrecy, the conflict between the county and the city stagnates. The city continues to wear black (a law is a law), and Görgei continues to stay away from the city (a threat is a threat). As a precaution, Görgei moves the county seat out of Löcse to his own estate. Meanwhile, the love between Rozália and Fabricius grows. Nustkorb, the new judge of Löcse, proves incapable (or, perhaps, reluctant) to carry out the city's vengeance against the deputy sheriff of the county. On rare occasions, and under the cloak of darkness, Görgei visits his daughter at an inn near the edge of the city. It is during one such visit that Nustkorb encounters Löcse's "enemy." Nustkorb fails to capture Görgei; instead, the deputy captures him. Görgei forcefully moves the judge to his own estate where he dines his "guest" in style and then releases him. When word gets out about this, the burghers' indignation is revived, but not so much against Görgei as against the intolerable standstill which continues to force them to officially mourn for their long dead judge and which has since spread their nickname, "the black city," far and wide. Nustkorb, more for the sake of making a move than for the sake of complying with some specific strategy, decides to bring to Löcse the statue of the dead judge that had been commissioned some time prior to his capture by Görgei. On the way back with the statue the wagon turns over and the statue falls on Nustkorb who is thus "murdered" by his own predecessor. When news of this apparently supernatural event reaches Löcse, its inhabitants feel that "the old judge has killed the new judge" (V, 428).

Indeed, the accident with the statue that results in the death of the new judge of Löcse revives the stagnant conflict. But now the townsmen seem less bent on revenge. In fact, two interpretations of the event (both endowed with supernatural significance) soon produce two factions. According to the first, the fact that the statue of the old judge has killed the successor of its original is a clear indication that Nustkorb is responsible for the death of the old judge from which it follows that " 'Görgei is not that guilty after all, therefore, it is time to stop wearing black.' " According to the reasoning of the second faction, however, the old judge has killed the new precisely because the latter has proved himself " 'ineffective in obtaining satisfaction for the dead. Therefore, it is now or never! Heaven itself is warning the City of Löcse' " to act without further delay (V, 456–57). The peaceful faction is headed by an old, respected townsman; the "militant ones" rally behind the young Fabricius (V, 457).

At this point Rozália sends a letter to her father requesting a secret meeting because she has something "important to communicate" (V, 461). What this something important is, is well known to the reader. Rozália would wish to receive her father's blessing for her upcoming nuptials with Fabricius. Meanwhile, however, a complication arises. Görgei's nephew, not realizing the attachment that exists between Rozália and Fabricius (since, at Rozália's request—and for reasons clear for the reader—the attachment has itself been kept in relative secrecy), also decides to ask for his cousin's hand in marriage. When Görgei learns of this, he is the happiest man on earth. Since his brother and sister-in-law (the nephew's parents) do not object to the marriage, this is proof conclusive that Rozália is his own daughter after all. The old suspicion, the suspicion that has never really given Görgei a moment's rest, is finally put to rest.

Hereafter the plot of the novel moves swiftly to its inevitable conclusion. The title of the last chapter is curiously reminiscent of the eighteenth-century novel: "In which against the will of the author and in accordance with the caprice of providence this history is concluded" (V, 463). I shall have more to say about the implications of this title later. At this point it is enough to trace the remainder of the plot which will itself indicate how carefully Mikszáth had worked out the tragic ending of his novel.

Certain political machinations and behind-the-scenes innuendoes move Görgei to return the county seat to Löcse. News reaches Görgei that the fact that the country officials have been meeting away from the city may produce undesirable misunderstandings between the local government and the Emperor. Görgei's decision to return to Löcse in an official capacity does not seem to produce any ripples in the city. The deputy's informants seem to indicate that all is quiet and that no harm would come to Görgei, even if he were to come to the city all by himself (V, 474). Rozália's eccentric "guardian" is the only person not satisfied with the apparent quiet. He thinks that the city officials have been behaving secretively of late, and he suspects that " 'an invisible wooden horse' " is being prepared.

As the narrator hastens to inform the reader, the old eccentric "was right" (V, 475). The night before the deputy's scheduled return to Löcse, a place of execution is built across from the City Hall. Fabricius, the new judge of Löcse and the leader of the "militant ones," is the mastermind behind the plot against Görgei. Görgei, who has just found conclusive proof that his daughter is his after all, becomes careless because he is so happy. He rides ahead of his retinue and enters the gates of the town only to find the gates close *after* him. He is soon overpowered and taken to the City Council where Fabricius passes judgment upon him. Görgei is to be executed without delay. It is not until immediately after the execution has been carried out that Fabricius learns Rozália's true identity from her frantic "guardian." The last sentence of the novel, spoken by an attendant at the City Hall, is simply: " 'Hurry, hurry, water, the judge has fainted' " (V, 492).

One of Mikszáth's critics makes much of the fact that Görgei and

Fabricius are of similar, almost identical, character: they share the same kind of nobility of heart and mind.[17] This is not entirely wrong, but there is evidence in Mikszáth's text for a significant distinction between these apparently similar characters that needs to be examined. Görgei, as representative of the nobility and of the county (as its deputy sheriff), is one kind of man of the law; Fabricius, as representative of the middle-class town dwellers and as city official and—later—judge, is another kind of man of the law. The difference between Görgei and Fabricius as "lawmen" is so significant that it makes their noble cast of mind (which they do have in common) quite insignificant by comparison.

Görgei's case in point occurs relatively early in the novel. It involves one of Mikszáth's most amusing anecdotes, one that involves a father marrying his own daughter-in-law after the latter's husband is believed dead, only to have the lost son return and find that his wife is now also his stepmother and that her children by his father are both his half-brothers and his nephews. This singular triangle comes to the deputy sheriff of the county for justice. From a legal point of view, the question can easily be settled, but Görgei proves to be of the old school of judges "who did not look into books when seeking for justice, but into the life situations of those who came to them for justice. . . . In those days apparently the judges were superior to laws . . . since then, it seems, the laws are better than the judges" (V, 186–87).

Görgei as judge, then, seeks justice not in terms of legal but in terms of moral rightness. He judges in terms of the situation and in terms of his own integrity. Not so Fabricius. Although the young townsman is interested in justice, and although his relentless pursuit of "justice" against Görgei is impregnated with a sense of idealism, Fabricius does not shy away from the kind of legalistic trickery which is almost by definition a betrayal of moral justice.

When, after hearing his death sentence, Görgei objects that the city has no legal jurisdiction over the county and, therefore, the deputy's execution would constitute murder, Fabricius refers to the *book* where it is stated that in the case of personal injury the injured one is to seek for justice from the authorities of the locality under whose jurisdiction the injury takes place. Since the judge of Löcse was killed on property belonging to the city of Löcse, the present judge of Löcse has a right to pass judgment on the deputy sheriff of the county (V, 488).

Yes, but the fact is that at the time of the "crime" in question the land where the incident occurred did not belong to the city; in fact, it is only because of the crime and of the victim's "friends" and colleagues that the land in question came subsequently under the city's jurisdiction. Of this the novel says nothing, but the careful reader will immediately notice that even if "legally" acceptable, the terms under which Fabricius claims to have a right over the deputy sheriff are, at best, highly dubious.

And there is more. When Görgei realizes that his execution is to be carried out instantaneously, he begs his judges to permit him to say farewell to his daughter. Fabricius once again, proves adamant with respect to a question of law: " 'whatever decision the council has passed, can never again be revoked' " (V, 490). In other words, Fabricius's stern legality will not even permit him this one small mercy.

The one decisive difference between Görgei and Fabricius, then, is that while the nobleman is guided by his own integrity, the townsman is guided by the integrity of the law. While, in the final analysis, Görgei makes himself responsible to himself, Fabricius evades responsibility in this sense by implying that his decisions are reached under the constraint of the law in whose service he functions. The title of the last chapter of the novel, according to which things happen "against the will of the author," can now assume a fuller significance.

In one sense the outcome of the story is clearly against the will of the author. Since the story is based on an actual event as it has come down to Mikszáth's time by a tradition of the then still extant Görgei family, the author has no choice but to remain true to the core of his novel's source (not that Mikszáth is not wont to change facts, but this is not the issue at the moment).

The outcome of the story is "against the will of the author" in a more important sense as well. Once the conflict between the county and the city is well under way, there emerges a new conflict, a conflict of universal significance, a conflict between a system where justice transcends the law and another system where the law transcends justice. Once the kind of system represented by Fabricius has a chance to determine the fate of the kind of system represented by Görgei, the outcome is inevitable. Even as "in politics appearance *is* reality" (V, 466, italics mine), in Fabricius's mind law *is* justice.

A fekete város is an open-ended novel. We never learn what happens after Fabricius's return to consciousness. The fact that he has lost it is, of course, in itself of some significance. When he learns that he has just killed the father of his bride-to-be, he must also realize in a flash what his own blind commitment to the law has made of him. He must, in other words, become conscious of his own tragic flaw. This new consciousness is of such unbearable force that its possessor must needs give it up temporarily. And Rozália? We never learn what happens to her hereafter; we never even see her receive news of her father's ignoble capture and execution. We can speculate that she will probably be taken in by the family of her father's brother; she will certainly never marry Fabricius now. The narrator does give us one hint of this. The night before the fatal day Fabricius whispers in Rozália's ear that he hopes they can meet on the next day, and at this point the narrator remarks that he "was so close to her and yet already so far, as though whole oceans had separated them" (V, 477).

Looking at the overall structure of the novel for a moment, the reader can see that Görgei's rash act of passion is responsible for the circumstances under which Rozália and Fabricius are to meet and fall in love, while Fabricius's calm act of legality is responsible for the irrevocable unmaking of their future together. By the end of the novel the petty, local conflict that has come and gone against the backdrop of a great historic moment that has also come and was soon to be gone, has swallowed up the potential happiness of a young couple. In the annals of the county or the city the whole conflict would be but a question of principle, a kind of reason for continued paper warfare where legal terms would jostle with one another for supremacy. The historic forces behind the conflict, then, which make the county-city contention seem trivial and futile, are themselves counterbalanced by the forces of personal tragedy.

In terms of the personal tragedy that strikes both Rozália and Fabricius, the petty, local conflict is neither petty nor local. And herein lies the greatness of Mikszáth's last novel, which is able to represent different levels of reality (the national, the local, the personal), each with its own significance and each with its own particular importance. It is, in the long run, as a result of the constantly shifting interaction among these different levels of reality that human destiny must fight for a chance while human nature must fight with itself and for itself that that chance may come to be the best rather than the worst possible chance. In this novel it becomes the worst. But in its meaning there resides a hope greater than the tragedy of its own action.

CHAPTER 5

Mikszáth's "Realism" in Perspective

I *Is the Realistic Mikszáth a Critical Fiction?*

THE specter of the Realistic Mikszáth has been one of the most persistent and problematic issues haunting Mikszáth criticism almost from the time of the first critical response to his work. The problem is intensified by the fact that Mikszáth himself seems to have flirted with the Realism (though not with the Naturalism) that came to dominate the international literary scene toward the end of the nineteenth century.

One of the first signs of Mikszáth's awareness of certain Realistic doctrines comes with his emphasis on "observation" at the expense of "fantasy" in "Galamb a kalitkában." As the original subtitle of this story indicates, the two narratives that comprise it are meant, among other things, to distinguish the Realistic and the Romantic precisely on the basis that the first is the product of the observer's eye while the second is the offspring of the teller's imagination. But as I have already shown (in Chapter 2, IV), the tongue-in-cheek authorial quarrels with projected or implied readers render Mikszáth's stance with respect to the two modes ultimately indeterminate.

The "Preface" to the 1889 *Almanach* is much more helpful in this regard in that here Mikszáth speaks in a straightforward manner of a "healthy realism" clearly in the making which manifests itself by virtue of the fact that a "writer is inspired by what he has seen rather than by what he has read" (XV, 708). This pronouncement is certainly in accord with one of the most clearly formulated tenets of Realism recorded as early as 1826 by an anonymous French critic who states that the new "literary doctrine" attempts a "faithful imitation not of the masterworks of art but of the originals offered by nature."[1] Mikszáth's pronouncement also implies that its author would be in wholehearted agreement with the notion that Realism involves a desire to abandon the metaphysics of Romantic Idealism on the basis that "reality [should] be viewed as something immediately at hand, common to ordinary human experience, and open to observation."[2]

Unfortunately, however, this probable agreement between Mikszáth and certain tenets of Realism cannot be taken for granted because Mikszáth himself seems to contradict it. In his "Preface" to the 1910 *Almanach,* written in praise of the educational value of fairy tales, Mikszáth speaks of "fantasy" as God's special gift to mankind (XV, 817). Another passage that modifies Mikszáth's supposed insistence on "observation" can be found in his "Epilogue" to *Jókai Mór élete és kora (The Life and Times of Mór Jókai;* 1905–06*)* where he claims to have sought not the "inert truth of a photograph, but the truth of the artist" (VI, 426).

By itself this is, of course, not in contradiction to any Realistic tenet; but as the previous chapters of this book have clearly indicated, Mikszáth's artistic truth is intricately and inseparably connected with his poetic vision of life. This vision, in turn, frequently pits the Romantic against the Realistic where the first is almost always associated with what is beautiful or desirable in life while the second is usually characterized by what is materialistic, selfish, or downright spineless. And whether the Romantic wins (as it does in *Szent Péter esernyöje* and *Különös házasság*) or loses (as it does, partly, in *Beszterce ostroma* and, completely, in *A fekete város*), the reader's sympathies are unquestionably enlisted on its side.

Evidence to the contrary notwithstanding, most of Mikszáth's critics seem obsessed with the idea of his Realism. For example, István Király, the author of the last full-length monograph to appear on Mikszáth to date, insists time and again that Mikszáth is either a Realist or moving toward Realism. He sees a significant and proportionate relationship between Mikszáth's changing political affiliations and his ever more Realistic criticism of the society of his age. According to Király, the more Mikszáth sees the corruption and the decadence of the once worthwhile Liberal Party, the more he moves away from Romanticism and the more he moves toward Realism.[3]

The implication in this, as well as the implication in other, similar statements, is that an author's Realism has less to do with his characteristic modes of perception than with his characteristic attitude about what is perceived. In other words, the form (which in

Mikszáth is almost never Realistic) is conveniently overlooked when it comes to the content or matter (which is frequently Realistic, that is, which is frequently critical of the way things are in Mikszáth's age). In the final analysis, however, Király can do no more than claim that "for Mikszáth realism did not mean a stubborn adherence to external, surface reality, but the creative imagination's careful liberation of the spirit of observed phenomena," and that the purpose of this "liberation" is to "reveal the internal, essential truth" of things and events.[4]

István Sötér also sees Mikszáth's Realism in terms of his changing political attitudes. In an essay on *Beszterce ostroma* he argues that prior to the writing of this novel Mikszáth is still the victim of his own illusions about the historic role of the nobility, and that in this particular novel we are the witnesses of a process of disillusionment which is, at the same time, a "strengthening" of Mikszáth's move toward Realism.[5] This, however, does not stop Sötér from seeing that the novel is composed of "contradictory elements," and that the scenes that take place inside the Pongrácz castle are not as Realistic as those that take place outside it.[6]

Writing about Mikszáth's poetics, Béla Illés, a more recent critic, states pointblank that Mikszáth "demanded that writers present a *true* picture of life and *true* portraits of man," that he himself dismissed idealized heroes but without accepting or advocating the other extreme, the extreme of "clinical studies" of despicable characters, for these are no more "true of the *whole* of life" than are the former.[7] Overlooking the fact that many of Mikszáth's characters *are* highly idealized (this is especially true of his heroines), and even characters such as Mihály Tóth in such otherwise Realistic novels as *Noszty fiú*, Illés simply reaches the rather tame conclusion that in the final analysis Mikszáth "favors" and "recommends" Realism.[8]

Two important essays appearing in the early 1960's take a much more sophisticated and tenable stance with respect to the whole question of Mikszáth's Realism. The first of these conceives of the whole question as a series of "problems" peculiar to Mikszáth, while the second places the word *Realism* in quotation marks in its title, thereby indicating that the Realism in question is fraught with difficulties.[9]

The first of these essays, Barta's, is an excellent and intelligent study of various "Mikszáth problems," and foremost among these is the problem of Mikszáth's Realism. This essay reopens a whole series of questions treated by Mikszáth's earliest critics (discussed in Chapter 1, of this book), namely, the relationship between folk and fairy tales and Mikszáth's Romantic vision of life, and the role of the "live" narrator assumed by most of Mikszáth's projected storytellers. Barta emphasizes the fact that in Mikszáth's novels the narrative voice plays a more prominent role (that it is more an integral part of the novels' overall effect on the reader) than in most novels that emphasize action or character, and that the narrator's apparent artlessness hides an artistic pose of the highest order. Because Mikszáth's readers are charmed, ultimately, by the author's own personality as it manifests itself in various and sundry narrative poses, the world presented by Mikszáth's novels takes on an authenticity and credibility that is the direct result of the underlying personality implied by their narrators.

But, Barta adds, this should not stop the reader from seeing that Mikszáth's novels are full of well-known (and frequently outmoded) conventions, and that this is true of such late novels as *Noszty fiú* where the heroine's disguising herself as a serving girl or the fortune hunter's disguising himself as a hunter can be seen as shopworn examples of certain traditional conventions. Barta concludes that Mikszáth is a "romantic realist."[10]

Mezei's essay, which is a direct response to Barta's, speaks of the various "Mikszáths" as in some sense the creations of Mikszáth's various critics.[11] Apparently somewhat unhappy with Barta's conclusion, Mezei attempts to place the Hungarian "realism" of the latter half of the nineteenth century in a historical perspective. He speaks of the end-of-the-century tendency to romanticize everyday life and the world of politics, and he concludes that the Realism of the age is at best a "medley" composed of elements from fairy tales and pictures of life as life is actually lived.[12]

In the end, Mezei sees Mikszáth's entire career as an uninterrupted struggle for the establishing of a "national" prose, as an attempt to "find the novel in the land of anecdotes." It is for this reason that in Mikszáth's works "motives as well as problems recur," and it is for this reason that the Mikszáthian world is ultimately accumulative in its effects. Mezei's conclusion is that Mikszáth's " 'humorous' works are born, as it were, against his own tendency to be well disposed toward report and naturalistic objectivity."[13]

The answer to the question posed by the title of this section, then, is by no means an easy or a simple one. There is a sense in which

Mikszáth's Realism is clearly a critical fiction, that is, there is a sense in which the critic's wishes to see Mikszáth as a "Great Realist" are imposed upon his works. Such critics as Király, Sötér, or Illés, for example, write almost as though they were determined to make Mikszáth the author of their own idea of Realism. Barta and Mezei, on the other hand, seem bent on making the whole issue seem more complicated and consequently more accurate than that (and rightly so), but they are still unwilling to relinquish the specter of Realism that clearly should not haunt Mikszáth.

Notwithstanding a few isolated and, ultimately, halfhearted pronouncements made in favor of certain Realistic tenets, Mikszáth's practice, as evidenced by my analyses of his novels in the preceding chapters, is decidedly unrealistic. But saying this is still saying something very problematic. I do not wish to imply that Mikszáth is anti-Realistic (though at times he is clearly anti-Romantic), for this would be false. At the same time it would be also false, or at least highly misleading, to imply that Mikszáth's world is not a frequently accurate representation of the world of late nineteenth- and early twentieth-century Hungary. Paradoxically this is most true, perhaps, of his most self-conscious and metafictional novel, *Két választás Magyarországon*. This raises a whole new question concerning the relationship between the fictive and the real, and of Mikszáth's implicit (and at times explicit) response to this question.

II *Mikszáth's Fictions about Fiction*

In speaking of "A gavallérok," Aladár Schöpflin—one of Mikszáth's earliest critics—mentions the fact that "Mikszáth loves characters whose lives are based on a lie in such a way that the lie emerges as their subjective truth." Later Schöpflin goes on to make a statement that surprisingly anticipates much later fiction and much relatively recent criticism: "When lies thus become an important ingredient in human life, the distinction between a truth and a lie, between what is real and what is imagined, itself becomes faint . . . [and this may give rise to the question that] if what is but the offspring of imagination can thus become true, is not what we take to be reality in general itself but the offspring of imagination?"[14]

There can be no doubt of the fact that Mikszáth's works abound in characters who live in fictions of their own making. But these characters do not fit into a single category. Count Pongrácz in *Beszterce ostroma,* for example, cannot be said to be the mere victim of his own imagination. On the surface he seems to be unaware of the difference between the age he is actually living in and the age he thinks he is living in. On a deeper level, however, it is clear that Pongrácz's choice of a quasimedieval world is based on his implicit recognition that the modern world is not an adequate stage for his life. The characters who hire a troup of actors to represent the "delegation from Beszterce" explicitly recognize that Pongrácz's life is an implicitly theatrical performance, a quasiartistic attempt to control reality.

The clash between different versions of reality is in fact familiar in many of Mikszáth's novels. The legend created by the old umbrella in *Szent Péter esernyöje* is explicitly shown to be a lie, but the "legend" is nevertheless more real than the simple reality which underlies it. In *Akli Miklós,* on the other hand, the "legend" of the hero's treachery is also a lie, but here it is the "truth" which is more real (and more "legendary") that captures the reader's sympathies. Sometimes the clash between different versions of reality is playful, as it is in *A szelistyei asszonyok* where the King's theatrical performance belies the truth in the same way in which the Transylvanian delegation's performance implies a truth that is in reality a lie. There are times, however, when the clash is irresolvable, as in *Új Zrinyiász* where the heroes of old remain incompatible with the modern ideas of and about the old.

But the Mikszáthian world of various characters, or classes, or whole societies living in fictions of their own conscious or subconscious making, is not exhausted by the characters, or classes, or societies themselves. The narrative voice bringing these various configurations of illusions intended to be mistaken for realities together with the various instances of self-delusions, makes itself felt at all times. The notion that "everyone sees with his own eyes, and judges and constructs according to his own mind" (VI, 422) is at once a clue and the interpretation of the clue.

In the long run, the subjective truth of a character is not only true for that character, it is also true for the reader. This is so because all truth is, in a sense, subjective. Where there is an identity between a subjective truth and the subjective interpretation that produces it, there is always a "good" character. The characters in "A gavallérok" or Pongrácz in *Beszterce ostroma* belong to this category. Where, however, there is a discrepancy between a subjective truth and the subjective interpretation that produces it, there is always an "evil" character. Akli's enemies, the Döry witnesses in *Különös házasság* and the Noszty clan in *Noszty fiú* all belong to this category.

Mikszáth's works, then, are conventional fictions about nonconventional fictions. They are in short artistic truths about the truths of life itself where the truths of life itself are themselves "made up," as it were, in a way not unlike the way in which the novelist's truths are also made up. What Mikszáth's works constantly imply (sometimes explicitly and sometimes implicitly) is that the difference between fact and fiction is not the difference between truth and falsehood, but the difference between the merely existent and the significantly human. This seems to lead to the apparent paradox that everything significantly human is a fiction; and so, for Mikszáth, it is.

But this does not mean that there are no distinctions between truth and falsehood. There are in Mikszáth true fictions, such as those of "A gavallérok" or of Pongrácz in *Beszterce ostroma,* and false fictions, such as those of Katánghy in *Két választás Magyarországon* or of the Noszty clan in *Noszty fiú.* In Mikszáth the reader seldom encounters a fiction that is neither true nor false in this sense. Görgei's suspicion that his real daughter is dead and that the girl supposedly his daughter is not really his is an example of this. Whereas most perpetrators of false fictions deliberately intend to deceive—that is, they deliberately intend their fictions to be mistaken for realities—, and whereas most perpetrators of true fictions are more or less self-conscious victims of their own wishful thinking, Görgei is simply the victim of man's fiction-making power. He is not deliberately abusing this power; he is merely unaware of its operation. For lack of a better term, this unawareness of the operation of man's fiction-making power may be called "total fiction."

These three subdivisions under the general heading of fiction, that is, true fiction, false fiction, and total fiction, are in some form or another constantly present in metafiction. According to a recent critic the "hallmark" of all metafiction is a "keen perception of paradox in the relationship between fiction and reality. . . . If human reality is itself a dizzying kaleidoscope of individually improvised fictions . . . a novel is a fiction at a second remove, a manifest fabrication about fabrications."[15]

This is most evidently true of *Két választás Magyarországon.* In that novel false fictions, the fictions of Katánghy and his kind, are clearly contrasted with true fiction, the fiction perpetrated by "Mikszáth" in the very act of writing the book, while total fiction applies to the characters within the novel who are duped by the various false fictions perpetrated by Katánghy or others. Here the reader is unquestionably in a privileged position. He sees what most of the characters in the book do not see, namely that Katánghy's fictions are false, but he also sees something else, namely that "Mikszáth" is writing a true fiction. From the reader's point of view, then, the difference between Mikszáth's novel and a historical work dealing with the same period would amount to a difference best summarized by the following: history is factual fiction; fiction, afactual history. It should be kept in mind that a distinction such as this is manifestly implicit in Mikszáth's work.

In the tongue-in-cheek "Preface" to the 1900 *Almanach*, Mikszáth explicitly addresses himself to this precise relationship between the fictive and the real. "Képzeletbeli miniszterek" ("Imaginary Ministers") takes up the playful contrast between the realm of the novelist and that of the journalist. The difference between the two is that while the novelist "works for immortality, the journalist works for tomorrow" (XV, 763). Mikszáth's subject matter in the "Preface," however, is not so much about the difference between these two realms, but about the difficulty of keeping them distinct. In order to accomplish the "impossible" feat of keeping these two "imaginary realms" separate, Mikszáth claims to require the services of two "imaginary ministers," one from each. These two ministers, however, are not always capable of keeping their respective realms from encroaching upon one another's territories. In fact, one or the other will at times deliberately create trouble for "Mikszáth" by giving the wrong kind of advice.

One such instance involves a story during the composition of which one of Mikszáth's imaginary ministers prompts the author to insert "a real name" in his fictitious text (XV, 767). Since the character bearing the real name is given an imaginary ring of great value, a member of the family pays a visit to Mikszáth soon after the publication of the story. This "relative" claims that other members of the family charge him with having unlawfully appropriated the valuable ring mentioned in the story. The "relative" requests that Mikszáth write a retraction of the entire episode. When Mikszáth responds that this will not be necessary since the story in question is " 'not history,' " since the ring is " 'imaginary,' " and since the whole episode is presented in such a way that it cannot possibly " 'be taken seriously,' " the complainer's simple response is to say that " 'that is all the more reason for my relatives to believe it completely.' "

Because of this "unpleasant" episode, Mikszáth calls upon his imaginary ministers and lays down the following law: "in novels no fictitious things shall be attached to real persons" and "in newspapers no real persons shall be given fictitious attributes" (XV, 768). But the attempt to abide by this law proves futile, for soon a politician mentioned in a newspaper article complains about a fictitious attribute *he* gives himself.

This tongue-in-cheek piece about imaginary ministers is Mikszáth's testimony that there are good reasons why the realm of the real and that of the fictitious are difficult to keep apart. Rather than speak of unrealistic "form" and Realistic or occasionally anti-Romantic "matter" or "content," it would behoove Mikszáth critics to speak of the world of his novels as making constantly implied distinctions between fiction as afactual history and accounts of real life (private or public) as factual fictions. The Realistic thrust, with the occasional utilization of certain tenets peculiar to late nineteenth-century Realism, of many of his works then would no longer demand that he be viewed as a "great Realist." And this would also make adequate room for the Romantic thrust more predominantly present in Mikszáth's work.

The term "romantic realist" is, in this sense, not misapplied, but perhaps "fabulator" would do better service here. Metafiction, or fiction about fiction, is of course the mode par excellence of the Mikszáthian fabulator. His afactual histories bear a significant relationship to the factual fictions of real life in that they are the fabulous displacements of the ways in which real life itself is consciously or subconsciously invented by those who actively or passively participate in it. All of Mikszáth's works seem, in short, to "demonstrate the necessity of making up 'fictions' if we are to understand and explain our own experience."[16]

But, as with all metafiction (and particularly so with Mikszáth's), the self-consciousness of fiction becomes an antidote for the unself-consciousness both possible and unfortunately frequent in real life. Self-consciousness is, after all, a form of self-knowledge, and self-reference is a form of self-scrutiny. Without these instances of awareness, the self runs the risk of totally eclipsing itself in unrecognized fictions of its own making. Mikszáthian self-consciousness is, in the final analysis, a constant warning to the reader: *de te fabula.* From Mikszáth's point of view, however, this Horatian admonition should be revised to: *actus fabulae fingendae de te,* for it is the act of making fables itself that concerns the reader.

CHAPTER 6

Conclusion

NO matter how eminent, there is a sense in which a Hungarian writer has no place in world literature. The school of thought that looks upon world literature from the point of view of Goethe tends to include in it the literatures of the major languages of the Western world, or, better, the literatures of the major nations. According to this school of thought almost nothing written outside of Russia, Germany, France, Italy, Spain, England, and the United States has a secure place in world literature.

There is, however, another school of thought usually, though not exclusively, advocated by the scholars of those nations that have been omitted by the above. In this sense world literature is, as the name implies, the literature of the world. It therefore seems advisable to speak of Mikszáth as having a place not so much in world literature as in the world *of* literature. Here he occupies an undeniably eminent position.

According to his life and times, Mikszáth's creative career falls roughly into the age of rising Realism and Naturalism on the one hand, and the coming of psychological and perspectival modernity on the other. He has, of course, more in common with Nikolai Gogol, Thomas Hardy, and Mark Twain than with Balzac, Emile Zola, or Theodore Dreiser. In "Legkedvesebb könyveim" ("My Favorite Books"; 1904), Mikszáth mentions that his immediate teachers included such foreign authors as Charles Dickens, Thomas Macaulay, and Thomas Carlyle. Among Dickens's novels *David Copperfield* seems to have left the greatest impression on Mikszáth. According to his own testimony, upon finishing that particular book he abstained from writing for a "period of three years" for fear of unfavorable "comparison." In this same piece Mikszáth acknowledges that his "simplicity of style" was directly influenced by the works of Macauley and Carlyle (sic). He also speaks here of a belated acquaintance with Dostoevsky, which came unfortunately at a time when its potential influence was no longer a possibility. "I was an old tree by this time," he tells us, "too old to grow in a different direction" (XV, 358). Among Hungarian writers, Mikszáth was most manifestly influenced by Jókai, the "Great Romanticist," under whose shadow he came to prominence and whose reputation he was not able to eclipse until after Jókai's death in 1904.

Nothwithstanding his reputation, partially self-generated, that he was a jovial and artless storyteller, Mikszáth was a deeply learned man. He read a great deal and at times he seems to have read relatively indiscriminately. A careful examination of his work, particularly of his quasihistorical novels, shows a great deal of research, though this research is never pedantic (except at times as a parody of pedanticism). Once an idea suggested by history becomes thematically significant, Mikszáth usually abstains from further research. Historic truth, in other words, takes second place to artistic validity. This is most manifestly true of such masterpieces as *Különös házasság, Noszty fiú*, and *A fekete város*.

His own influence on his followers is perhaps less evident than the influence he himself received. I am, of course, not speaking here of his conscious imitators. Nevertheless, without his deintoxication of Romanticism such of his followers as Gyula Krúdy, Ferenc Herczeg, and (above all) Zsigmond Móricz would not have had an easy time overcoming the necessary obstacles that could well have impeded their own development.

In the final analysis, however, Mikszáth's place in the world of literature is more important than either the immediate influences upon him or his own immediate influence upon his followers. In his work there is a strange mixture of eighteenth-century self-consciousness and early twentieth-century modernity. Were it not for the at times uncompromisingly doctrinaire insistence upon "social realism" in post–World War II Hungary, Mikszáth's continued influence would have necessarily produced unique native offshoots of such recent developments as the French *nouveau roman*. The quasisolipsistic self-consciousness of a Nabokov or a John Fowles or a John Barth could have also found a more fertile ground in present-day Hungary as a direct result of the heretofore neglected metafictional significance of Mikszáth's work. As it is, his vision of life combined with his particular embodiment of that vision is still awaiting a potential influence in a hopefully more open and more tolerant future. His works are there, and they speak a language of their own, and that language happens to be one of the major languages in the world of literature.

Notes and References

(Place of publication is Budapest unless otherwise indicated. All quotations from Mikszáth's works are in my own translation. All citations from primary sources are included in my text followed by appropriate volume and page numbers, and all refer to *Mikszáth Kálmán munkái*, 15 vols. [1965–70]. Other references to Mikszáth's works are included in the notes with the words *Critical Edition* preceding the appropriate volume and page numbers, and these refer to Gyula Bisztrai and István Király, eds., *Mikszáth Kálmán összes müvei*, 68 vols. [1956–73].)

Chapter One

1. For this highly simplified historic account, I am most indebted to the following: Paul Ignotus, *Hungary* (New York, 1972), pp. 57–106; Dominic G. Kosáry and Steven Béla Várdy, *History of the Hungarian Nation* (Astor Park, Fla., 1969), pp. 127–91; A. C. Macartney, *Hungary: A Short History* (Edinburgh, 1962), pp. 155–207; A. J. P. Taylor, *The Habsburg Monarchy: 1809–1918: A History of the Austrian Empire and Austria-Hungary* (London, 1948).
2. For this highly eclectic biography of Mikszáth, I am most indebted to the following: István Király, *Mikszáth Kálmán* (1952); Mózes Rubinyi, *Mikszáth Kálmán élete és müvei* (1917); Aladár Schöpflin, *Mikszáth Kálmán* (1941); Béla Várdai, *Mikszáth Kálmán* (1910).
3. *Critical Edition*, XXIV, 148.
4. *Ibid.*, p. 149.
5. *Ibid.*, p. 171; italics Mikszáth's.
6. *Ibid.*, p. 173.
7. Béla G. Németh, "Mikszáth Kálmán," *Türelmetlen és késelkedö félszázad* (1971), pp. 204–15.
8. Tamás Dersi, *Századvégi üzenet* (1973), p. 130.
9. Quoted by Schöpflin, p. 115.

Chapter Two

1. See Elemér Császár, *A magyar regény története*, Revised Edition (1939), p. 375; Várdai, p. 113.

2. Schöpflin, p. 132.
3. Rubinyi, pp. 38–39.
4. Géza Kenedi, "Irodalmi pletyka," *Az Újság*, 8, no. 121 (1910), as quoted by *Critical Edition*, VI, 203.
5. Rubinyi, pp. 55, 57, 91.
6. Schöpflin, pp. 105, 124.
7. Rubinyi, p. 68; Schöpflin, p. 138.
8. Várdai, p. 118; Schöpflin, p. 49.
9. Várdai, p. 90.
10. Schöpflin, pp. 15, 16.
11. *Ibid.*, pp. 38–39.
12. Király, pp. 53–54.
13. For a slightly different view of this form of narration see István Sötér, *Romantika és realizmus* (1956), especially pp. 561 and 565–66; also Kálmán Kovács, "Mikszáth Kálmán," *A magyar irodalom története* (1965), IV, 753, where Kovács refers to it as "gossip-like narration."
14. Rubinyi, p. 67.
15. Várdai, p. 91.
16. Schöpflin, p. 14.
17. *Ibid.*, p. 15.
18. Rubinyi, p. 25.

Chapter Three

1. Almost every critic whose evaluation of the novel is summarized in the notes to the *Critical Edition* makes mention of the similarities between Pongrácz and Don Quixote. See *Critical Edition*, VI, 259–93.
2. For an account of the historic bases of the novel see *Critical Edition*, VI, 199–232.
3. *The World of Don Quixote* (Cambridge, Mass., 1967), see especially pp. 25 and 109–11.
4. Kovács, p. 729.
5. The first English translation of this novel was apparently one of Theodore Roosevelt's favorites. At one point the President of the United States had even paid a visit to Mikszáth in Budapest to tell him so. See *Critical Edition*, VII, 291.
6. Király, p. 146.
7. Kovács, p. 721.
8. The story of Katánghy's marriage is apparently based on the marriage of a Polish doctor in Gleichenberg, Austria, as recorded by Sándor Závory in his memoirs (1914). See *Critical Edition*, IX, 188.
9. Joseph Reményi, *Hungarian Writers and Literature* (New Brunswick, N.J., 1964), p. 11.

10. For an account of the religious significance of *Szigeti veszedelem* see D. Mervyn Jones, *Five Hungarian Writers* (Oxord, 1966), pp. 8 and 21; Tibor Klaniczay, *Zrinyi Miklós* (1964), p. 155.
11. Király, p. 131.
12. Kovács, p. 723.
13. *The Dark Interval: Towards a Theology of Story* (Niles, Ill., 1975), see especially pp. 105 and 124–25.

Chapter Four

1. For a detailed account of the historical background with a generous sampling from the pertinent documents, see *Critical Edition*, XIII, 179–281.
2. Király, p. 168.
3. According to accounts of the "real" Buttler-Döry story, one claims that the marriage in question was forced, but it was only subsequently that Buttler met and fell in love with a Mária Buday who (unlike her novelistic counterpart) was to marry twice while waiting for the annulment to come through. Another account of the "real" story claims that the marriage in question was not forced at all and that it was only after a number of trial separations that Buttler attempted to have it annulled. For these conflicting stories see the recollections of Dezsö Bernáth and Gábor Bosits as quoted by *Critical Edition*, XIII, 186–95 and 195–202, respectively.
4. For a sampling from this reaction see *Critical Edition*, XIII, 251–75.
5. Reprinted in Béla Illés, ed., *Mikszáth Kálmán ars poeticája* (1960), p. 268.
6. Kovács, p. 738.
7. Gyula Ortutay, ed., *Magyar népmesék* (1960), III, 192–94. This tale is also available in English under the title of "A Deal That Went to the Dogs." See Linda Dégh, ed. *Folktales of Hungary* (Chicago, 1965), pp. 168–70.
8. Király, p. 196.
9. Kovács, pp. 723 and 724.
10. Quoted by *Critical Edition*, XX, 266.
11. Kovács, p. 745.
12. *Ibid.*, p. 753.
13. Király, p. 190.
14. Kovács, p. 753.
15. For a summary of the family chronicle on which the novel is based see *Critical Edition*, XXII, 246–49.
16. Kosáry, *History of the Hungarian Nation*, pp. 79–85. See also Ignotus, *Hungary*, pp. 38–39.
17. Kovács, p. 755.

Chapter Five

1. Quoted by René Wellek, *Concepts of Criticism* (New Haven, Conn., 1963), p. 227.
2. George Becker, "Modern Realism as a Literary Movement," *Documents of Modern Literary Realism*, ed. George Becker (Princeton, N.J., 1963), p. 6.
3. Király, pp. 112–13.
4. *Ibid.*, p. 246.
5. Söter, p. 557.
6. *Ibid.*, pp. 559, 570.
7. Illés in introductory essay to *Mikszáth Kálmán ars poeticája*, p. 13; italics Illés's.
8. *Ibid.*, p. 14.
9. János Barta, "Mikszáth-problémák," *Irodalomtörténeti Közlemények*, 65, nos. 2–3 (1961), 140–61 and 299–321; József Mezei, "Mikszáth és a század 'realizmusa,'" *Irodalomtörténeti Közlemények*, 65, no. 4 (1961), 448–69.
10. Barta, p. 313.
11. Mezei, pp. 450, 452.
12. *Ibid.*, pp. 455, 457, 460.
13. *Ibid.*, pp. 468, 469.
14. Aladár Schöpflin, "Mikszáth Kálmán," *Magyar irók: Irodalmi arcképek és tollrajzok* (1919), p. 51. This essay was first published in 1910.
15. Robert Alter, *Partial Magic: The Novel as a Self-Conscious Genre* (Berkeley, 1975), pp. 129–30.
16. Brian Wicker, *The Story-Shaped World: Fiction and Metaphysics: Some Variations on a Theme* (Notre Dame, Ind., 1975), p. 33.

Selected Bibliography

(Place of Publication is Budapest unless otherwise noted.)

PRIMARY SOURCES

1. Collected Editions

Mikszáth Kálmán munkái, 33 vols. Révai, 1889–1908.
Mikszáth Kálmán munkái, 32 vols. Jubileumi kiadás, Révai, 1910–17.
Mikszáth Kálmán összes müvei, 68 vols. Kritikai kiadás. Eds. Gyula Bisztrai and István Király. Akadémiai Kiadó, 1956–73.
Mikszáth Kálmán müvei, 15 vols. Magyar Helikon, 1965–70.

2. Individual Editions
(This section includes the most important works that appeared in Mikszáth's lifetime. Dates refer to first editions in book form.)

Novels
Nemzetes uraimék: Mácsik, a nagyerejü. Révai, 1884.
A két koldusdiák. Révai, 1886.
A beszélö köntös. Révai, 1889.
Szent Péter esernyöje. Légrády, 1895.
Beszterce ostroma: Egy különc ember története. Légrády, 1896.
Nagyságos Katánghy Menyhért képviselö úr viszontagságos élete, kalandjai, szerencsétlensége és szerencséje. Révai, 1896.
Prakovszky, a siket kovács. Légrády, 1897.
Egy választás Magyarországon: vagy, A körtvélyesi csiny. Légrády, 1898.
Új Zrinyiász: Társadalmi és politikai szatirikus rajz. Légrády, 1898.
Különös házasság, 2 vols. Légrády, 1901.
A szelistyei asszonyok. Légrády, 1901.
Akli Miklós cs. kir. udv. mulattató. Légrády, 1903.
A vén gazember. Révai, 1906.
Jókai Mór élete és kora, 2 vols. Révai, 1907.
A Noszty fiú esete Tóth Marival, 3 vols. Franklin, 1908.
A fekete város, 3 vols. Franklin (?), 1911.

Stories

Elbeszélések, 2 vols. Wodjáner, 1874.
Még újabb fény- és árnyképek. Grimm és Horovicz, 1878.
Az igazi humoristák. Szeged: Endrényi, 1879.
A tót atyafiak. Grimm Gusztáv, 1881.
A jó palócok. Légrády, 1882.
Az apró gentry és a nép. Révai, 1884.
Úrak és parasztok. Révai, 1885.
A fészek regényei. Singer és Wolfner, 1887.
Club és folyosó. Révai, 1887.
A tekintetes vármegye. Révai, 1889.
Pipacsok a búzában. Révai, 1890.
Tavaszi rügyek. Révai, 1890.
Galamb a kalitkában. Singer és Wolfner, 1891.
A kis primás. Révai, 1892.
Kavicsok. Petöfi Társaság, 1893.
Pernye. Révai, 1893.
Az eladó birtok, Páva a varjúval. Singer és Wolfner, 1894.
Kisértet Lublón és egyébb elbeszélések. Légrády, 1896.
A gavallérok, Ne okoskodj Pista. Légrády, 1898.
A fekete kakas és még három elbeszélés. Légrády, 1901.
Öreg szekér, fakó hám. Légrády, 1903.
Mikor a mécses már csak pislog. Légrády, 1903.
Vilagit este a szentjánosbogár is. Révai, 1906.

English Translation

A Strange Marriage, trans. István Farkas. Corvina Press, 1964.
"The Gentry" (a translation of "A gavallérok"), *Hungarian Short Stories*, ed. A. Alvarez. London: Oxford University Press, 1967.
Prakovszky, the Deaf Blacksmith, Hungarian Short Stories, ed. István Sötér. Corvina Press, 1962.
St. Peter's Umbrella, trans. B. W. Worswick. Corvina Press, 1962. This translation was originally published in London by Jarrolds and Sons in 1900.

SECONDARY SOURCES

1. Books

KIRÁLY, ISTVÁN. *Mikszáth Kálmán*. Müvelt Nép Könyvkiadó, 1952. Well-written monograph that emphasizes the political influence on Mikszáth's works.

RUBINYI, MÓZES. *Mikszáth Kálmán élete és müvei*. Révai, 1917. Good critical and biographical work by an eminent Mikszáth scholar, with a useful bibliography of uncollected material.

———. *Mikszáth Kálmán stilusa és nyelve*. Révai, 1910. Somewhat pedantic account of the various stylistic and linguistic qualities of Mikszáth's prose.

SCHÖPFLIN, ALADÁR. *Mikszáth Kálmán*, Franklin, 1941. Highly readable biographical and critical work, with special emphasis on Mikszáth's poetic vision of life.

VÁRDAI, BÉLA. *Mikszáth Kálmán*. Franklin, 1910. Excellent early account of Mikszáth's development as a writer. Avoids personal life of the author.

2. Articles

BARTA, JÁNOS. "Mikszáth-problémák," *Irodalomtörténeti Közlemények*, 65, nos. 3–4 (1961), 140–61 and 299–321. Excellent and highly insightful modification of Mikszáth as "Realist."

CSÁSZÁR, ELEMÉR. "Mikszáth Kálmán," *A magyar regény története*. Revised Edition. Királyi Magyar Egyetemi Nyomda, 1939, pp. 361–70. Good general introduction to Mikszáth the novelist.

DERSI, TAMÁS. "Mikszáth is segit," *Századvégi üzenet*. Szépirodalmi Könyvkiadó, 1973, pp. 130–32. Brief but highly amusing account of the provenance of *Szent Péter esernyöje*.

ILLÉS, BÉLA. "Mikszáth ars poeticája," *Mikszáth Kálmán ars poeticája*, ed. Béla Illés. Szépirodalmi Könyvkiadó, 1960. pp. 5–25. Good general summary of Mikszáth's ideas about writers and literature.

KOVÁCS, KÁLMÁN. "Mikszáth Kálmán," *A magyar irodalom története: 1849–1905*, ed. István Sötér. Akadémiai Kiadó, 1965, IV, 702–61. Excellent and rather detailed general introduction with intelligent interpretations of most major novels and some major stories.

MEZEI, JÓZSEF. "Mikszáth és a század 'realizmusa,' " *Irodalomtörténeti Közlemények*, 65, no. 4 (1961), 448–69. Another excellent contribution to the problematic question of Mikszáth's "Realism" with special emphasis on the historical difficulties surrounding the development of Realism in Hungary.

———. "Új 'balgaságok története': Mikszáth," *A magyar regény*. Magvetö Könyvkiadó, 1971, pp. 382–411. A somewhat hybrid but brilliant general introduction with special emphasis on Mikszáth's thematic preoccupations.

NÉMETH, G. BÉLA. "Mikszáth Kálmán," *Türelmetlen és késlekedö félszázad*. Szépirodalmi Könyvkiadó, 1971, 204–15. Interesting but ultimately highly questionable discussion of the various stages of Mikszáth's development.

REMÉNYI, JOSEPH. "Kálmán Mikszáth: Novelist and Satirist," *Hungarian Writers and Literature*. New Brunswick, N.J.: Rutgers University Press, 1964, pp. 154–64. Good general introduction with remarkable detail in view of its brevity.

SCHÖPFLIN, ALADÁR. "Mikszáth Kálmán," *Magyar irók: Irodalmi arcképek és tollrajzok*. Nyugat, 1919, pp. 30–54. Well-considered early essay with special insights with respect to the world of fiction and its thematic significance in real life.

SÖTÉR, ISTVÁN. "Mikszáth Kálmán és a *Beszterce ostroma*," *Romantika és realizmus: Válogatott irodalmi tanulmányok*. Szépirodalmi Könyvkiadó, 1956, pp. 253–72. Good account of the Romantic and Realistic elements in the first of Mikszáth's important novels.

SZERB, ANTAL. "Mikszáth Kálmán," *Magyar irodalomtörténet*. Révai, 1947, pp. 412–15. Brief but invaluable introduction to Mikszáth in general. Remarkably detailed in view of its brevity.

Index

(The works of Mikszáth are listed under his name)